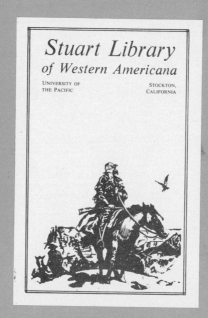

The BANDIT BELLE

Carl W. Breihan is the author of many Western books, among which are:

"The Complete & Authentic Life of Jesse James"
"Badmen of the Frontier Days"
"Quantrill and His Civil War Guerrillas"
"The Day Jesse James Was Killed"
"Younger Brothers of Missouri"
"Great Gunfighters of the West"
"Great Lawmen of the West"

The BANDIT BELLE

By Carl W. Breihan
with
Charles A. Rosamond

The story of the notorious
BELLA STARR combined with
other tales of almost legendary
characters . . . The life story
of HENRY STARR (written by
himself while in prison) . . .
True facts about "HANGING
JUDGE PARKER" and his
hangman GEORGE MALEDON
. . . CHEROKEE BILL
and others.

HANGMAN PRESS
As Presented By
Superior Publishing Company

Of Seattle, Washington

FIRST EDITION

DEDICATED TO

Lawrence K. Roos, Supervisor,
St. Louis County, Mo.

And to my fellow colleagues on the
St. Louis County Council

Milton J. Bischof, Jr.

Brainerd W. La Tourette, Jr.

John O'Hara

Maurice W. Osborn

Gerald A. Rimmel

Maurice L. Stewart

and the Council's
Administrative Director

Edward L. Sprague

&
Staff

TABLE OF CONTENTS

Bronze figure of Bella (often miscalled "Belle") by Jo
Mora in Woolaroc Museum.

CHAPTER 1

Bella Starr,

Oklahoma Whirlwind

They called her in two ways. One was "Cherokee Maiden" but the moniker didn't fit. She was no Cherokee and she certainly was no maiden — not by any conception of the word. The other was "Queen of the Bandits," a title as fit as any. Spiteful, reckless, headstrong, somewhat beautiful, as dangerous as any of the desperadoes she loved and as lusty as a woman can be, Bella Starr was as romantic and colorful a figure as the west produced.

She married an Indian half her age in full tribal ceremony and was, ironically, a ward of the United States Government at the height of her outlaw career. In later years she joined forces with Henry Starr, a distant relative of her husband, who once boasted he had held up more banks than any other man in history. He was the only man who ever pulled off two bank stickups in the same town on the same day, and he was killed attempting to stick up a bank in the grand old tradition of the frontier — just three years after the close of World War I. In her day, Bella Starr's forest hideout provided safety for some of the most famous outlaws of all times. And yet when legend and rumor are stripped away, hers is probably one of the most vicious of all western biographies.

Great pains have been taken to check the actual place and birth of Bella Starr. Many contemporary newspapers claim she was born at Georgia City, Missouri on February 3, 1846. Members of various bandit families say she was a native of the Kentucky hills. The noted author, S. W. Harmon, says she was born February 3, 1846 in Carthage, Missouri, while another biographer, Burton Rascoe, is less specific saying she was born prior to 1848 in Washington County, Missouri.

Although most writers agree with the month and the day, February 3rd, some have placed her birth as early as 1844. The United States Census records of 1850 and 1860 give the true information. Page 397, R. 518, 1850 clearly states that Myra Shirley was born in 1848, February 5, the date inscribed on her tombstone. The census of 1860, Page 827, R. 441 shows her to be 12 years old, clearly establishing the birth year as 1848. It also states that her place of birth was Jasper County and that in 1860 she lived in Marion Township, Carthage, Missouri. She was not actually born in Carthage, but at a point called Medoc, Missouri, ten miles away. The town was later renamed Georgia City. It appears fairly certain, therefore, that she was born in Georgia City, Missouri on February 5, 1848.

Christened Myra Maybelle Shirley, she later changed her middle name to Bella (not Belle) on a whim of her own. Her father, Judge John Shirley (the judge being an honorary tile only) was a farmer and showed real estate at about $600 at the time of Bella's birth. Her father's birthplace is somewhat vague although census records list the State of Virginia. Little is known about her mother except that she was believed to be Elizabeth Hatfield, related to the feuding Hatfields of West Virginia-Kentucky, and that she went by the name Eliza. As to the rest of the family there is also conflict. Her favorite brother and undoubtedly Edwin Benton (called Edward by some writers) was 11 years old in 1860, although some say he and Bella were twins. Census records also show Charlotte A. Shirley, 12 years old in 1850 and John Allison Shirley, 8 years old in 1850. In 1860 there were two more, Mansfield, 8 and Cravens, age 2. The four brothers were born in Missouri and Charlotte was born in Iowa.

In 1860 the Shirleys lived in Carthage, where the judge owned a hotel. He had prospered considerably with real estate listings of $4,000 and personal property of $6,000. The Carthage Hotel stood on the spot now occupied by the Carter Hardware Company and bore the glaring sign:

CARTHAGE HOTEL
NORTH SIDE PUBLIC SQUARE

John Shirley, Prop.
Horses and Hacks for Hire.
A Good Stable Attached.

Young Bella was educated at the Carthage Female Academy where she was well liked and considered a very pretty girl. Little is known about her brothers except Edwin, who was called Bud. It was Bud Shirley who probably exerted a stronger influence on Bella Starr than any other person. Bud was still a youngster when he took up arms against the Federal troops and joined Quantrill's raiders. Some say he was a captain but he was far too young. Others claim he was also a member of General Jo Shelby's Iron Brigade, but it appears likely that he remained with Quantrill except for a brief period when he roamed as a freebooter of so-called southern sympathizers, looting and burning under the guise of patriotism.

Bella early earned her reputation as an expert horsewoman riding to Bud's defense. It was in 1863. Bud was visiting his home in Carthage after serving as a guerrilla for some months and the Federal troops were in constant pursuit. Through the guerrilla grapevine Bella learned that Bud's presence in Carthage was known and Union troopers had been dispatched to arrest him.

The young girl was in Newtonia, some forty miles away, when she got the news and she planned to ride to Carthage in order to warn her brother. The Federals under direction of Major Eno, however, also had Bella under surveillance and arrested her, keeping her in custody until they were certain she could not reach her brother in time to assist him. They were wrong. On her release, Bella made a wild dash across the rugged countryside, taking to unbroken trails, galloping through creeks and gulleys, and actually outdistanced the Yankee troops. When the soldiers arrived, Bud Shirley had made good his escape.

Some writers have taken great pains to discredit this wild ride, but the concerted efforts of the Federal authorities in Missouri to apprehend Bella meant she was giving them a lot of headaches.

A year later in the summer of 1864, Young Shirley's luck ran out. He and a companion, Milt Norris, were surprised at the home of Mrs. Stewart near Sarcoxie, Missouri, and Bud was shot to death attempting to make his escape by scaling a fence. Norris escaped and raced to Carthage to tell the Shirley family.

The soldier who killed Bud Shirley was a member of the 15th Missouri Cavalry, Company C, but his name has been lost to the records. A few days later Bella, only 16 years old at the time, rode into Sarcoxie with two heavy revolvers strapped around her waist and announced she was there to avenge her brother. No one knows whether she found the Union soldier and had her revenge, but it is generally conceded that the incident was a springboard which launched her career as a lady bandit. Rumor has it that Bella, who had ridden into Quantrill's quarters on occasion to deliver messages, now dressed herself like a man and rode with the marauders. The story seems doubtful since the only record of any woman riding with Quantrill is that of Kate Clark, a young girl practically kidnapped by the vicious Quantrill, who became part of his gang and later set up a bawdy house in St. Louis with money given her by the guerrilla leader.

Among the friends of young Shirley was Jim Read (erroneously spelled Reed in some accounts), the son of a wealthy Missouri farmer. Soon after the death of young Bud, Judge Shirley and his family left Missouri and moved to Dallas, Texas, where the elder Shirley owned a ranch. Shortly after they had moved from the state, Carthage was burned to the ground by Federal troops, the Carthage Hotel and Shirley house being among the buildings destroyed. It was at the Dallas ranch that Jim Read courted Bella and finally married her. It has been reported that this marriage was performed while Bella and Read sat on horseback and that "Bloody Bill" Anderson, one of the more vicious of Quantrill's raiders, held the bridles, with the aid of one John Fisher. Twenty other horsemen witnessed the wedding performed by a Justice of the Peace. There seems to be some doubt as to the legality of the ceremony, as it is known that the judge and Mrs. Shirley objected to the wedding. Doubts have also been voiced as to the truth of reports on the wedding. It is certain that Anderson played no part since he was killed two years before near Orrick, Ray County, Missouri, and his head was sliced off and stuck on a telegraph pole.

In later years Bella said she married Read because he killed the soldier who had slain her brother, and she had vowed to marry the man who avenged Bud's death. At any rate, Judge Shirley did everything in his power to separate the two. Twice they hid her from the brigand, and twice he came and took her away. Finally the Shirleys sent Bella to a relative in Colorado. But Read followed her there and took her back to Missouri with him. The following year, 1869, a girl was born to the couple in Missouri. She was named, Rosa Lee Read and apparently was given to Read's mother to raise. She was later known to history as Pearl Younger.

It was as Read's wife that Bella's life of crime really began. Hot tempered and without conscience after his days with Quantrill, Read soon was on the run from the law. Jim's younger brother got in a fight at a horse race in Fort Smith, Arkansas with a man named Fisher. A gunfight followed. The younger Read was accidentally shot to death by a man named Shannon, who lived on a ranch next to the Reads. Despite the fact that most people were convinced that the shooting was accidental, Read sought out Shannon and killed him. Bella and Jim raced across the border into Indian Territory, a refuge for outlaws and killers because they were immune to arrest except by United States Government officers.

It was while in hiding that Bella first saw the handsome young Sam Starr, son of Tom Starr, a prominent Cherokee Indian scout who was letting the Reads use his tepee as a home. Read was uncomfortable even in the sanctity of the Indian

lands, so they left for California shortly, Bella and Pearl making the trip by stagecoach and Jim traveling on horseback. Life in California was good to them. They were happy there, took several trips to Mexico, and in 1871 their second child, a son, was born. They named him Edwin after Bella's slain brother.

It was inevitable that Read would fall afoul of the law, however, even though this time he was apparently an innocent victim of circumstances. He was arrested for passing counterfeit money, and the officials were about to release him on the charge when they learned he was wanted in Fort Smith for murder.

Read was out on bond and when the officers went to rearrest him, they found he had fled their jurisdiction. Read headed back to the Shirley ranch in Texas while Bella took the long trip around Cape Horn. Jim probably made the journey on horseback although there is no record concerning this part of the trip. Bella dressed Pearl as a boy so that the authorities would not become suspicious of her. By the time Jim and Bella were together again at the Scyene farm, the judge was reconciled to the marriage, mainly because he had two grandchildren.

In Texas, Bella assumed her role of a shady lady in grand style. She opened a gambling hall in nearby Dallas while Read remained in the background, helped by people who knew of his southern sympathies during the Civil War, and were glad to keep him shielded from the law on the Shannon murder charge. The Younger brothers lived near the Shirley home and Bella was frequently seen in their company. Women of the day whispered about the flashy young Read woman who paraded down the main street in her daring clothes, and dealt faro in the gambling house.

When Jim was arrested on some minor charge by a deputy sheriff named Nichols, Bella openly bragged that she was going to kill the lawman. Shortly afterwards Nichols was shot to death in the street. There were no witnesses to the killing, and despite Bella's threats she was not arrested in connection with the shooting.

Read was released from jail since Nichols was the only witness against him on the other charge; the state had no case with their witness dead. Whether Bella actually shot Nichols or not is strictly a matter of conjecture. She was certainly capable of the act and did not stand short on courage. Once when Read was in jail she went to visit him. Inside the cell they quickly switched clothes, and Read walked out dressed like a woman. Legally they could have held Bella for aiding and abetting a criminal, but the law was too busy with other matters in the dissention-torn South to bother. She was released without charge.

Wanted by the law, Read turned to his old profession, banditry, riding with a band of gunmen through the Territory and adjacent states. But while many accused him of outlawry, others believed that he was a kind of misspent Robin Hood, robbing from the rich and giving to the poor. In 1873 a crime was committed which turned even the most ardent sympathizers against Read. Jim was recognized as one of the band which went to the home of Watt Grayson, a wealthy Indian, reputed to have a large sum of gold hidden on his premises. Grayson was beaten; then tortured by the thugs, but refused to divulge the hiding place of the money. The thieves finally turned to his squaw and tortured her until she told them where the gold was. Under the house they found $30,000.

Some reports state that Bella was a member of the band, while others say she was in Dallas at the time. In all fairness to her it must be reported that in 1875 it was learned that the other two men with Read during the Grayson affair were Dan Evans and Sam Wilder. Evans himself confessed this when he was later arrested for the murder of a cowboy named Seabold of McKinney County, Texas in 1873. He was hanged for this crime of murder on September 3, 1875 at Fort Smith. Wilder, in the meantime, had already been arrested for another crime and was serving time in the penitentiary at the time Evans was hanged.

At any rate, the Grayson robbery turned the full wrath of the local people against the Reads. Bella sprouted out with a full string of race horses, running them in races throughout Texas, but she was socially ostracized by the people. The long arm of the law, meanwhile, stretched towards Read. He was killed shortly afterwards in what Bella later described as "one of the most treacherous deeds ever perpetrated in the annals of infamy."

Some accounts state that Read was cut down by Texas Rangers and stated on his deathbed that he had participated in the Gads Hill train robbery in Missouri with Jesse James, and in the Austin-San Antonio stage holdup. Here is what actually happened:

Soon after the Grayson robbery Read drifted to Paris, Texas, where he met John Morris. Read, always willing to help a friend in trouble, loaned Morris $600 after his friend lost all his own money in a high stakes poker game. Several days later Morris and Read, riding together, stopped at the home of Charles Lee, 15 miles from Paris, Texas, where they had breakfast.

Before entering the house, however, Morris suggested they place their pistols in the saddlebags so as not to appear discourteous or suspicious. Read took off his sixgun and put it in the bag with his friend's weapon. Morris finished his meal first and then walked to the back door where he suggested to the host that they kill Read and share the nice reward. The two men shook hands on the deal. Morris went outside, got both guns from the saddlebag, and came back into the house just as Read was finishing his meal. With both guns cocked, Morris demanded that Read surrender to his custody.

"Damn you, villain, treacherous coward!" screamed Read. "I'll die first!"

"Then die!" cried Morris.

Read leaped to his feet and Morris fired the first shot. The bullet slammed into Read's chest but he did not fall. Grabbing a heavy wooden table, he upended it and rushed Morris, using the piece of furniture as a shield. Morris fired several shots through the top of the table but Read kept coming. As he approached Morris, the assassin sent another slug splintering through the wood, and Read toppled over with a bullet in his heart. Although some people reported that Morris sneaked up behind Read and shot him in the back, Bella and Mrs. Shirley both verified the first report at the time of the shooting. Record shows that Read died from a bullet fired into his heart from a frontal angle and not from through the back.

Morris claimed $1700 in rewards, but the money did him little good. He was killed shortly thereafter at his ranch near Ft. Worth, Texas. The tavern keeper received $300 for his minor role in the assassination of Bella Starr's first husband. It is not known whether Bella had anything to do with the death of Morris or not. When she received the news of Read's murder she dropped to her knees, and overcome with grief, swore in the presence of God to avenge the death of her husband. Those who knew Bella later stated that her grief was due more to rage than to actual sorrow. At any rate, she berated the remainder of the Read family for not taking up arms against Morris. There were rumors at the time that she even refused to identify the body of her husband to keep Morris from receiving the reward, although it is doubtful she ever saw the body, and it seems certain now that Morris did get his blood money.

Bella's reputation had suffered immensely during her flamboyant Dallas days, and the rampages of Jim Read before he was killed. It became manifest in the fact that old Judge Shirley, a once respected member of the community, even paid for her wickedness. Bella returned to her father's farm in Scyene soon after Read's death, and found the family virtually blacklisted by the entire community. In 1876 Judge Shirley died and was buried in an unmarked grave in a nearby cemetery. Efforts to locate the grave have been fruitless. Bella's mother, heartbroken at the death of her husband and the contempt suffered by the family because of her daughter's exploits, moved back to Missouri.

In 1876 Bella opened a livery stable on the outskirts of Dallas, and rumors began to spread that local outlaws were seen there frequently. The stable soon was suspected as a storeplace for stolen horses, with Bella acting as a "fence" for the animals. The James brothers and the Youngers among them stopped off at Bella's place at times. People began to speak of Bella Read in whispers behind their hands, saying that she frequently visited the homes of strange men for other than livery stable business. She once acquired $2500 in one lump sum from a wealthy cattleman named Patterson. Why she got it is anyone's guess, but she used the money to send her two children to school at Rich Hill, Missouri, the home of Read's mother.

In 1878 Bella was finally arrested for having stolen horses in her possession. In no time she landed in a Dallas jail. Never one to stand long on ceremony, Bella flirted with a deputy and soon had him eating out of her hand. He helped her to escape and even accompanied her, but he was back a few days later — tied to his horse with a note pinned onto his badge, "Returned for unsatisfactory reasons." Yes, that was like Bella, all right.

Bella's list of lovers was long and impressive. She even circulated the rumor that she was at one time married to Cole Younger, the noted Missouri outlaw. These reports were further bolstered by the fact that Pearl Read sometimes went under the name of Pearl Younger. Others said she was married to Bruce Younger, a rugged miner who lived at Galena, Kansas, a rough and ready mining camp of that day across from' Joplin, Missouri. Some writers say Bruce was Cole Younger's brother, others that he was a cousin. Records show that Bruce Younger actually was a half-brother to Cole's father, and was the black sheep of that family. Living relatives of Cole confirm these findings. Later Bruce Younger married an Indian girl,

but there is no record of any bethrothal to Bella. Investigation also produces another Bruce Younger, age 18 in 1850, and the son of Coleman Younger, Liberty Township, Clay County, Missouri, who was 40 years old at that time. This Bruce in fact was a cousin of the bandit, Cole Younger, but his name Bruce is preceded by the initial "C." There also are no records of this Bruce having wed Bella. There is, of course, plenty of reason to believe that Bella perhaps did have an affair with one of these men. It was not uncommon in those days for a woman to claim to be a man's wife without going through the bothersome formality of a ceremony.

Another on Bella's list was a man named Blue Duck. He was an Indian outlaw leader. Bella was queen of this gang for a while. We have no other record of this outlaw's name other than Blue Duck, which is the English translation of his Indian name.

The gang rustled cattle, horses and raided small banks and held up stages in the Indian Territory. Bella was a fiery and demanding figure of "royalty" in this desperado empire. Once while riding on the prairie, Bella's hat flew off. When Blue Duck made no effort to retrieve it, Bella drew her revolver and promptly demanded a little respect. Her lover quickly fulfilled her wish, got her hat and they continued on their ride. But if she was harsh in her demands for courtesy, Bella was just as efficient when it came to playing her part in the gang. Blue Duck on one occasion dipped into the outlaw brood's treasury and skipped into Dodge City, Kansas with $2000 for a little gambling. He dropped the whole two thousand. The next night Bella appeared at the gambling hall, gun in each hand, and lifted the entire house bankroll. She made quite a profit. Her take was $7000. On the way out she informed the aghast owner that she didn't have time to count the loot, but if she got more than Blue Duck had lost he could bounce on over into Indian Territory and collect his change. There is no record of the owner bouncing over.

Her affections for Blue Duck seemed genuine. On June 23, 1884 her lover was arrested for the murder of a young man named Wyrick. Suspected of the murderous deed were Blue Duck, William Christie and Martin Hopper, the latter a relative of Blue Duck, and on whose farm the Wyrick boy had been killed. Immediately following the murder, Blue Duck disappeared, but Hopper was arrested and brought in for questioning. However, the authorities were unable to hold Hopper due to insufficient evidence.

Shortly after William Christie was arrested on a charge of peddling whiskey in the Territory. The authorities did not wish to alert Blue Duck by charging Christie with the murder of Wyrick, so they made their prisoner a proposition. If Christie would lead the lawmen to Blue Duck's hideout they would drop the whiskey peddling charges against him. Eager to jump at such a chance, the perfidious Christie led the officers to the hideout. There Blue Duck was promptly arrested and he and Christie were taken to Fort Smith, where Blue Duck was questioned.

During the course of this investigation, circumstances were brought to light which implicated William Christie in the murder of Wyrick, and he was held over for the Grand Jury. That body, however, failed to indict him, so he was permitted to return home.

Failing to keep their promise to Christie about the whiskey peddling charge, he was arrested by the officers, brought to court and sentenced to the county jail for a year. While serving his term, Christie was again investigated by the Grand Jury, indicted and held on a murder charge, along with Blue Duck.

At the trial the first man to take the stand was William Christie. He testified that on the day Wyrick was slain he and Blue Duck were at the home of a man named Ross, some three miles from the Hopper residence and that all of them were drunk. Further stated that after leaving the Ross home he and Blue Duck went to visit Hopper, but found him not home, so they decided to wait for him. Christie claimed that when Mrs. Hopper went to the spring for a bucket of water he rested on the porch and dozed off, and did not awaken until he heard five pistol shots fired in rapid succession. Also stated that he was alone and that when he sat up he saw Wyrick's plow horse coming dashing into the yard, and that he caught the animal and tied it to the fence. Christie further claimed that at the time Blue Duck approached he was carrying Martin Hopper's revolver in his hand and that the gun was empty.

When placed on the witness stand Mrs. Hopper repudiated Christie's statement, stating that when she appeared shortly following the shots, Christie was holding the pistol and not Blue Duck. Also that he took six cartridges from a cartridge belt and gave them to Blue Duck, telling him to reload the weapon. At that time Blue Duck mounted his horse and left.

Hawky Wolf testified that Blue Duck came to his home and fired a shot at his son, Willie Wolf,

and three shots at himself, all of the bullets missing. Also that Blue Duck had told him he had just killed Wyrick over at Hopper's place. Evidence also was brought out that neither Blue Duck or Willie Christie was armed at the Ross place. If neither man was armed at the Ross house, how did Blue Duck come into possession of Martin Hopper's pistol, and where did Christie obtain the full belt of cartridges for the weapon — unless Hopper had a hand in the crime?

Blue Duck denied all the evidence submitted. Martin Hopper dodged the law and was not present during the proceedings. "Hanging Judge" Parker's court found Blue Duck guilty, but William Christie was acquitted.

Blue Duck didn't have a chance in Parker's court and neither did any other criminals brought before that bench. Judge Parker had been appointed Federal Judge for the District Courts for the Western District of Arkansas with criminal jurisdiction over the Indian Territory on August 10, 1873 by President U.S. Grant, and he really took his work seriously. In the more than 20 years he served before dying in office November 17, 1896 Hanging Judge Parker disposed of no less than 88 men on his gallows. Needless to say Blue Duck got the limit. Tried in 1885, Blue Duck was convicted on January 30, 1886, and sentenced on April 30th, the date for his execution set as July 23, 1886.

No one gave Blue Duck much of a chance after that, since anyone given such a sentence in the court of Judge Parker seldom did not hang. But Bella Starr did not rest a minute. She engaged the legal services of the famous J. Warren Reed, and raised enough money to take the case out of Judge Parker's hands. They went direct to the President of the United States, and finally were able to have Blue Duck's sentence commuted to life imprisonment.

"There's no prison in Arkansas that will hold that Indian," were the words on everyone's lips, so Blue Duck was taken to the Southern Illinois Penitentiary at Menard. The records there say that he was not married. There he remained a prisoner until March 20, 1895, when he was pardoned and left the prison a free man. It was not long after that he became involved in a fatal disagreement in a Kansas gambling palace and ended up in the local cemetery.

After Blue Duck had been lodged in the Menard Prison, Bella sped back to Indian Territory, to the home of her husband, Sam Starr, son of Tom Starr, and whom she had married on June 5, 1880, according to the official records of the Canadian County, Cherokee Nations marriage reports.

Shortly before that time Bella had come to the Starr tepee and cast an amorous eye upon young Sam Starr. Matrimony was soon in the air, much to the dismay of the elder Starr, who did not approve of his son's marriage to a woman nearly twice his age. But soon Bella and Sam were united in a strict and sacred Cherokee tribal wedding, as well as by Abe Woodall, District Judge for the Canadian District, Cherokee Nations. And, strangely enough, when Sam took Bella as his wife, the United States Government, by law, took her as a ward, so the bandit lady actually was now the government's full responsibility.

This seemingly had little effect on her conduct or on Sam's. With her handsome Indian husband Bella took up a thousand acre claim on the Canadian River near Eufaula, Oklahoma, and moved into a log cabin which was standing there. They named the location "Younger's Bend," a somewhat romantic name for the new bride to pick considering her past experiences with some of the Youngers. Bella decorated the walls of the dim little abode with colored linen she purchased on frequent trips to St. Louis. Bella also became quite the fashion plate in this period of her life. She took up the side-saddle, apparently because it was the accepted way for a lady to ride in Europe, and she created quite a figure dashing about on a specially made saddle which appropriately was called the "Starr Saddle."

Younger's Bend became a popular meeting place for some of the most notorious outlaws of the day. The low-slung, tiny cabin witnessed many outlaw revels which included the appearance of members from the former Jesse James gang. A popular rumor that the bandits hid their loot near the cabin created a furor in later years, and people flocked to the scene with shovels, virtually plowing up the whole area in search for the ill-gotten riches. None of it was ever found. The robbers of the day just didn't bury their loot like the old time sea pirates, they simply spent it as fast as they stole it. Stories even circulated that Cole Younger once made a stop at the house after a man said he saw an outlaw wearing those famous hand-made leather boots with "C.Y." branded into them, around the place. The story is false, the boots with those initials might have been seen, but Cole Younger certainly was not wearing them. Cole was arrested in 1876 and was in prison years before Bella ever moved to the Bend.

Rumors of the happy and unlawful days at Younger's Bend eventually reached the ears of Judge Parker, and the Hanging Jurist sent a posse of deputies out to arrest the whole lot. A friend of the Starrs was waiting when the lawmen arrived, telling the group that the former occupants had moved away. The deputies left without a search; Bella and Pearl, who were hiding inside, returned to their chores.

Parker was not to be denied, however. Shortly after their first visit to Younger's Bend, officers of Parker's court paid a second visit, this time arresting Sam and Bella on a charge of horse theft and possession of liquor, a Federal offense in the Indian Nations. The Starrs claimed they were framed and Parker apparently believed them. They were given relatively light sentences of one year each in the Detroit, Michigan House of Correction.

There has been varied opinion on what happened to Pearl Read during her mother's incarceration at Detroit. Some say she lived with a family named McLaughlin in Parsons, Kansas, and others say she stayed in Oswego. In a letter from Bella to Pearl, reference is made to "Mamma Mac," which might well be Mrs. McLaughlin. The letter was sent to Oswego, Kansas and was first published by the noted western authority Harmon, in 1899. He claimed it was genuine and it appears to be. It seems a well written letter for Bella to compose, but she did have a fair education and then, too, the original letter might have been edited by someone else along the line.

My Dear Little One:

It is useless to attempt to conceal my trouble from you and though you are nothing but a child I have confidence that my darling will bear with fortitude what I now write.

I shall be away from you a few months, baby, and have only this consolation to offer you, that never again will I be placed in such humiliating circumstances and that in the future your tender little heart shall never again ache, or a blush called to your cheek on your mother's account. Sam and I were tried here, Jim West, the main witness against us. We were found guilty and sentenced to nine months at the House of Correction, Detroit, Michigan, for which place we start in the morning.

Now Pearl, there is a vast difference in that place and a penitentiary; you must bear in mind, and do not think of mama being shut up in a gloomy prison. It is said to be one of the finest institutions in the United States, surrounded by beautiful gardens with fountains and everything nice. There I can have my education renewed, and I stand sadly in need of it. Sam will have to attend school and I think it is the best thing that ever happened for him, and you must not be unhappy and brood over our absence. It won't take the time long to glide by, and as we come home we will get you and then we will have such a nice time.

We will get your horse up and I will break him in, and you can ride John while I am getting Loco. We will have Eddie with us, and will be gay and happy as the birds we claim at home. Now baby, you can either stay with grandma or your Mama Mac, just as you like and do the best you can until I come back, which won't be long. Tell Eddie that he can go down home with us and have a good time hunting, and though I wish not to deprive Marion and Ma of any length of time, yet I must keep him a while. Love to Ma and Marion.

Uncle Tom has stood by me nobly in our trouble, done everything that he could do. Now baby, I will write you often. You must write to your grandma and don't tell her of this; and your aunt Ellen, Mamma Mac, but to no one else. Remember, I don't care who writes to you, you must not answer. I say this because I do not want you to correspond with anybody in the Indian Territory. My baby, my sweetheart, my little one, and you must mind me. Except Auntie – if you wish to hear from me, Auntie will let you know. If you should write me, Ma would find out where I am and Pearl, you must never let me know. Her head is overburdened with care now, and therefore you must keep this carefully guarded from her.

Destroy this letter as soon as read. As I told you before, if you wish to stay a while with your Mamma Mac, I am willing. But you must devote your time to your studies. Bye, bye, sweet baby mine.

Belle Starr.

There has been some question raised as to the authenticity of this letter by those (including this writer) who point out that Bella usually signed her name with the "a" – Bella and not Belle. It is also noted that she did not sign the letter "mother," which should have been proper in this case. It is also seen that Bella referred to her sentence as nine months when actually she got a year. This letter was supposedly written to Pearl in February of 1883, shortly before Bella left for Detroit, how did she know she was going to serve only nine months before she was paroled. Besides, why was the letter not destroyed?

On the other side of the ledger, there are folks who claim they saw Bella write and mail the letter at Fort Smith. It was addressed to Pearl at Oswego, Kansas. A member of the Robinson family at Joplin, Missouri stated he saw Pearl Read living at a hotel in Parsons, Kansas in 1882 or 1883, and that the hotel was operated by a family named McLaughlin.

On release, the Starrs returned to Younger's Bend with Pearl and a Mabel Harrison, an orphan Bella brought with her from Missouri. The two girls attended school at Briartown, and for a while things at the Bend seemed quiet and happy. Sam, however, had already had his taste of quick riches, and the law was soon on him again, this time for a post office robbery. He fled to New Mexico. A short time later Bella was under indictment for stealing horses again. She certainly did not live up to her promise to Pearl about going straight. The following item appeared September 20, 1886 in the Little Rock, Arkansas *Gazette:*

Ft. Smith, Sept. 18 – Bella Starr, who is here on bond awaiting trial, has received word from her home on the Canadian River stating that her husband, Sam Starr, who had been dodging officers for several years, has been badly wounded in a conflict with the Indian Police. Bella said her information was that police fired on and wounded Sam, killing his horse, without demanding his surrender and that fifty shots had been exchanged in the fight. Bella has the court's permission to be absent until next Wednesday, and will leave in the morning for her husband's bedside.

Apparently Sam's wounds were not as bad as the item intimated. He regained consciousness in the sheriff's office where he was taken after the shooting, seized a guard's gun and escaped. When Bella returned to Younger's Bend she found him hiding in the brush. It appeared that Bella was beginning to tire of running. She advised her husband to surrender, and he returned to face a court.

Sam Starr was arraigned and trial was set for March 7, 1887. He was released on bond and with his wife, Pearl and Mabel, started for the Bend to await the court proceedings. Enroute they stopped at the home of Lucy Surratt to relax. A dance was in progress and one of those present was Frank West, one of the possemen who had fired on Sam. Witnesses stated that as Sam entered the room and saw West he drew and fired without warning. Mortally wounded, West fell to the floor but managed to pull his gun and fire back. When the smoke cleared Bella Starr was again a widow.

The charges against Bella were dropped after the death of Sam Starr, and once again she returned to Younger's Bend. For several months after her husband's death, Bella threw in her lot with Henry Starr, a relative of her late husband, who carried out a series of small raids and bank robberies in the Territory and adjacent states. There were rumors that Bella became a co-leader of the Starr gang but these were never founded. Starr was probably the last of the great frontier bank robbers. His association with Bella, however, was short.

Bella soon began to appear at carnivals, state fairs, and in theatres, making a living as one of the leading attractions of the day. Her daring exhibitions of marksmanship and riding attracted crowds from miles around, and she frequently took part in a sham stagecoach holdup in which the boisterous Hanging Judge Parker played the role of a passenger.

In 1887 Bella learned that Pearl was pregnant. Although Pearl told her mother she had married a half-breed Cherokee boy in 1886 in a ceremony prescribed by white laws, Bella had the young Indian run out of the Territory. There is evidence that Pearl fled to the home of the Reads in Rich Hill and had her baby. However, by using forged letters and trickery, Bella brought Pearl back to the Bend, and had the child admitted to an orphanage. At any rate, Pearl never saw her baby again. It was the general opinion that Bella seriously mistreated her daughter, virtually keeping her a prisoner at Younger's Bend.

In 1887 Pearl married a Cherokee Indian named Nilly or Jim July, but the vicious-tempered Bella refused him admittance until he changed his name to Starr. Edwin Read also had turned bad and was considered a trouble-maker and a bully. In her attempts to straighten the youth out, Bella often bull-whipped him mercilessly. The boy openly hated his mother, even threatening at times to kill her. It appeared that Bella, embittered after her long years on the wrong side of the law, and the loss of two husbands and several lovers, was now trying to regain some semblance of respectability. Her efforts were to little avail, however. Jim July was a horse thief, and was later shot to death by United States Deputy Marshal Bud Trainer in Choctaw Country. Edwin was killed while shooting up a saloon in Wagoner in 1896.

In the late 80's a man named Edgar Watson moved into a farm on the south side of the Canadian, River about seven miles from Younger's Bend. Watson appeared to be a law-abiding man, and merchants with whom he dealt expressed the utmost faith in his integrity and honesty. Bella had wormed her way into Watson's confidence, however, and learned that he was suspected of murder and was wanted in Florida.

The Kansas City *Star* on April 10, 1910 in an item on Bella Starr gives a description of Bella's murder. The paper also intimates that Watson and

July were engaged in stealing horses, and Watson had refused to make a fair division of the spoils. Bella had threatened to betray him.

On Sunday, February 3, 1889 Bella rode into King Ranch store and gin, and told the proprietor she had come to eat dinner with him. The previous day Bella had accompanied July part way to Fort Smith, where he was going to answer a horse theft charge. She was riding her favorite mare, a fast, spirited animal. At dinner she appeared worried and apprehensive, and told the guests there that she had a premonition of death. She was laughed at and the comment was made, "thunder and lightning couldn't kill you."

Before she left the ranch Bella snipped a large silk handkerchief in half; gave half of it to a tenant farmer's wife as a keepsake, and left a cloak for which she had paid $40 with the store proprietor for safe keeping.

Bella left the store at 1:00 P.M., and before reaching the river stopped at the home of a man named Barnes, where she passed the time talking with the women until about 3:00 P.M. When she arrived there Watson was standing in the back yard with a shotgun. He left at once in the direction Bella would travel. Bella left after getting some corn pone from Mrs. Barnes. At 4:00 P.M. Mike (Frog) Hoyt, a farmer, was crossing the river on a ferry when he heard a rapidly running horse coming through the underbrush. He saw Bella's riderless mare leap from an embankment into the river and swim across. Hoyt rode back up the road. At a sudden turn in the trail his horse pulled up short and snorted. The body of Bella Starr lay in the middle of the wooded trail.

Bella was killed with two loads of mixed shot from a shotgun. She apparently had been shot in the back and had fallen into the road with her face in the mud. While lying there unconscious, her assassin walked up beside her, took her own revolver from its holster and shot her in the head. The weapon was then replaced.

Most of the local residents believed that Watson was the killer. Tracks led from the scene to a point near his home. There were those who thought that perhaps Ed or Pearl had exacted their toll of vengeance for the mean way in which Bella had treated them and that one of them had been responsible for her death. Watson was arrested, but was released on lack of evidence. Later he found his way to the Island of Chokoloskee in the Florida Everglades where they meet the Gulf of Mexico. This island was used by outlaws and deserters during the Civil War, and for most part was seldom visited by anyone. Watson proclaimed himself "emperor" of the island and ruled for a number of years. On October 24, 1910 a handful of honest fishermen shot and killed Watson on the boat landing at the store of Ted Smallwood. He was first buried at Rabbit Key and later reburied in the Fort Myers Cemetery. So passed the man of whom it was said: "He killed the famous Bella Starr."

Bella was dressed for burial by the women in the neighborhood. Her grave was dug in the dooryard and she was buried without a prayer, a pistol in her right hand. Some sensationalists have claimed that this revolver was once the property of Cole Younger. Her grave was marked by a rough stone wall two feet high, with two large slabs tilted over the top in a "V" shape. The stone was carved by Joseph Dailey, a local stonecutter, whose name appeared in the lower left hand corner of the original stone. The grave is on the Bella Starr Ranch (Younger's Bend), thirteen miles from Eufaula, Oklahoma. The tombstone, ironically, was paid for by Pearl Read with money earned in the Pea Green Bawdy House at Fort Smith.

The original headstone was inscribed:

BELLE STARR
Born in Carthage, Mo.
Feb. 5, 1848

DIED
Feb. 3, 1889

Shed not for her the bitter tear
Nor give the heart a vain regret,
'Tis but the casket that lies here,
The gems that filled it sparkles yet.

Bella's daughter, Pearl Read, died in Douglas, Arizona, on July 8, 1925 and was buried in Calvary Cemetery, that city.

Today it is almost impossible to locate the exact spot of Bella's grave, and it is accessible only by foot or by jeep. We do know that one day someone opened the grave and removed the pistol that had been placed in the dead hand of Bella.

Strange as it may seem, no one in Eufaula had ever seen the grave of Bella Starr. At Porum, Oklahoma, on the Canadian River, it was learned that Claude Hamilton had taken over the grave property and some surrounding acreage in a back tax sale. It is such a desolate and forlorn spot that none ever visit it. Mr. Hamilton, seeing that roaming cattle had broken some of the grave marker stones, rescued them and placed them in a safe place, keeping them for another day's use. Perhaps one day a stream of tourists will pass the spot and gaze in wonderment at the grave of Bella Starr, just as they now do at the grave of Missouri's Jesse James and at the last resting place of other famous frontier characters.

The several people who do know the grave's location are keeping silent about it, hoping it will one day be a great tourist attraction. Until then, however, the remains of the once colorful Bella Starr, a woman who loved attention and notice, lies in an unmarked grave — gone but not forgotten, the grave now covered with stone slabs and surrounded by a wire and wooden fence and overrun with weeds and poison ivy.

* * * * * * * *

William Tuttle "Bill" Cook was the leader of as daring a band of outlaws who ever operated in Indian Territory. He was not a cold-blooded killer as many of the outlaws were, but confined his activities to robbery. Bill was born near Fort Gibson on December 19, 1873, and grew up as a farm hand and cowboy; sometimes he participated in the activities of a posse now and then, chasing bandits. In the spring of 1894 Bill's brother was accused of horse stealing, thus casting a light of doubt on his honesty also. In June of 1894 he organized a band of outlaws consisting of himself, Cherokee Bill, Henry Munson, Curtis Dason and others. He and his men were trapped at the Half Way House on Fourteen Mile Creek, where a gun battle ensued, with one of the possemen being killed.

It was too late for Bill to turn back after that. He and his men committed many bold robberies in the Cherokee and Creek Nations. On January 11, 1895, Bill Cook was arrested by Sheriffs T. D. Love of Borden County, Texas, and C. C. Perry of Chaves County, New Mexico, in a sod house of an isolated cattle ranch a few miles from old Fort Sumner, New Mexico. He was tried before Judge Parker in Fort Smith, being arraigned on twelve counts of robbery. On February 12, 1895, he was sentenced to a term of forty-five years in the Federal prison at Albany, New York.

* * * * * * * *

Bella Starr in her wild youth — all photos never before published. At left, as she appeared when running spy letters for Quantrill.

(Above) Bella Starr as working outlaw in 1889. (Right) Jim Read, one of Quantrill's Raiders during Civil War, became Bella Starr's husband and later bandit. One of his robberies was of the Austin-San Antonio Stage in April, 1874.

Bella Starr and her Indian outlaw paramour, Blue Duck.

Ed Reed, right, son of Bella Starr and Will Clark.
Credit photo University of
Oklahoma Library.

Guns used by Bella Starr in her stormy career. Top left, .36 cal. percussion Manhattan revolver; top right, Colt's single action .45; below, Colt's Frontier model and holster.

(Above) Bella Starr's home at Younger's Bend. It was here Jesse James told her the Youngers were captured in Minnesota. (Below left) Rare photo of Blue Duck, one of Bella's lovers. (Below right) Jim July, husband of Bella's daughter Pearl, but whom Bella named Starr.

Rear of Starr house. Outlaw visitor and his saddle horses, ready for quick getaway.

(Left) Trail where Bella Starr met death by shotgun blast.
(Below) Well at the Younger's Bend house.

BELLE STARR
Born in Carthage Mo.
FEB 5, 1848.
DIED
Feb 3, 1889

hed not for her the bitter tear,
Nor give the heart to vain regret;
Tis but the casket that lies here,
The gem that filled it sparkles yet.

J. Da

(Right) "Flowery" epitaph on Bella Starr's headstone.
(Below) Her grave as it originally appeared. Buildings
have disappeared, grave occupying inconspicuous spot in
pasture near Porum, Oklahoma.

(Above) Pioneers in Oklahoma Territory, 1888. (Below) South side of Main Street, Ellsworth, Kansas.

CHAPTER 2

The Starrs Against The Law

By Carl W. Breihan with Chas. Rosamond

Some write them heroes,
some very knaves.
Curses and tears are mingled
at their graves.

Ramon F. Adams's famous bibliography of Western literature, *Six-Guns & Saddle Leather,* lists this autobiography of Henry Starr as being published in 1914; a thrilling story concerning the life of Henry Starr, famous Cherokee Indian outlaw, who narrates his many adventures from boyhood to the date of his writing the manuscript. He lists the small original booklet as "exceedingly rare" and justly so. A quarter of a century of fruitless search finally ended in Chas. Rosamond locating a copy of this interesting paperbound booklet. The scarcity of the book is readily understandable; in fact, famous researchers of Western Americana failed to even realize that it existed at all. The late Martin Ismert of Kansas City, a noted collector and authority on things western, often said, "there ought to be some kind of a book done about Henry Starr."

Therefore, it is our good fortune and privilege to offer this exact facsimile of the original edition to the public, as well as a brief history of Bella Starr, a cousin of Henry Starr through marriage, and a number of photos of these two Starrs and their times.

The distinction of this little volume lies in the fact that Henry Starr himself wrote it, without the help of ghost writers, newspapermen or other assistance. He presents the facts of his life in a conscientious manner, without fictional elaboration, colorful inventions or apologies for his actions. Think what a monumental thing it would have been had such men as Jesse James, Cole Younger, Doc Holliday or Wyatt Earp kept diaries of their actions or wrote an autobiography such as Henry Starr eventually did!

Unlike the Jameses and the Younger Brothers, for instance, Henry Starr has been missed by all the historians of the West, even the semi-fictional publications specializing in the stories of bandits and banditry, such as *The National Police Gazette* and *The Chicago Ledger,* passed him by for some reason. Probably they were unaware of his dubious fame or did not research thoroughly. Yet he and his men were the only outlaws in history who robbed two banks on the same day in the same town and got away with it.

Yet, it is understandable in a way that Henry Starr's little book went by the wayside unnoticed by most people. It appeared at a date when the newsbutchers no longer sold their lurid novels of the western outlaws in the train coaches all over the country. This, too, possibly is the reason why the true story of Henry Starr has never reached the movie screen. In fact, we have no record that this story ever appeared on the screen, in any shape or form. And, as truth is stranger than fiction, it would make an exciting movie about an exciting outlaw.

The span of time does not alter facts and figures, yet it does tend to dull the enthusiasm of men who are noted writers in their field when it pertains to grass-root research and telling their stories in an unbiased manner. Even the famous Burton Rascoe, author of *Belle Starr, the Bandit Queen,* criticized William McLeod Raine's when he wrote in his fine work *Famous Sheriffs and Western Outlaws* that Frank Dalton, as a Deputy United States Marshal, was killed in the line of duty near Fort Smith, Arkansas when he tried to make a legal arrest. This is a fact as we have copies of the telegram sent to the Attorney-General in Washington giving an account of the fight and also the reply from his office offering a reward for the capture of the person or persons responsible for Frank Dalton's death.

We cite this one incident because we feel certain that no one will be able to discredit accurately this autobiography of Henry Starr. We say this because there are no other books about him that can be compared with his. To be sure, several articles have appeared relative to the life of Henry Starr, but most of this was taken from contemporary newspaper accounts and from old stories that may not be one hundred percent reliable. Many stories about Bella Starr have appeared in hundreds of publications, some of these items partially true; most of them totally in error except for proper names, dates and placés. The story of Bella, which also appears in this volume, we feel to be as accurate as can be at this late date, as well as being an appropriate history to include in this autobiography of Henry Starr.

On the other hand, we feel that more information ought to be imparted concerning Henry Starr, so a tedious task of research was begun to bring this about. Therefore, we wish to include a bit of Starr history as a conclusion to this introduction.

While some outlaws were driven to their misdeeds at the outbreak of their bandit lives; and given an opportunity to return to society, and failed to do so, for the majority of the badmen, robbery was the basic motive of their choice of livelihood.

On June 5, 1893 the Bentonville, Arkansas bank was held up and robbed of $11,000 or more in gold by a band of screaming and shooting horsemen. This bit of Monday crime was first attributed to the brain-work of one Jim Dyer but at the trial this assumption was disproved. Actually the five horsemen who rode into Bentonville at 2:30 in the afternoon were led by Henry Starr, then known simply as an Indian Territory desperado. The raid was not exactly a new experience for some of the older citizens of the town, for shortly after the Civil War, Jesse James and some of his men entered town and raided the store of Craig and Sons.

Two of the outlaws remained outside the bank to guard against a surprise attack by more courageous citizens, while the remainder of the band entered the bank building. There they compelled the bank officials to place their money in two grain sacks; one for the gold and currency and one for the loose silver. To add insult to injury, the bandits forced an assistant cashier to start carrying the heavy bag of silver to where their horses were waiting. As he passed one of the offices in the building, one Miss Maggie Wood opened her office door and grabbed the cashier and jerked him into the room. The robbers did not hesitate in their flight but raced to their mounts and hurriedly left the city. They were followed for several miles by a resolute posse which fired many shots in the direction the outlaws had taken, but the bandits managed to escape unharmed. But for two of them, Henry Starr and "Kid" Wilson, their liberty was short-lived. Shortly after the Bentonville robbery they were captured in Colorado Springs, Colorado, and jailed later on at Fort Smith, Arkansas.

It was the keen observance of William Feuerstine, a resident of Fort Smith, that brought about the arrest of the two outlaws, rather than the work of peace officers. Feuerstine was attending to some private business in Colorado Springs when he saw Henry Starr on the streets, recognized him and informed the police. An investigation of the city hotels revealed that on Saturday, July 1, 1893 Henry Starr, a woman, and Wilson had registered at the Spaulding House, using the names of Frank and Mary Jackson and John Wilson of Joplin, Missouri.

The officers realized that if they wished to capture these two desperate men without bloodshed or loss of life, they would have to act diligently and carefully. On Tuesday morning the police noted Starr and Wilson enter the Oppenheimer Store, where they bought some expensive items and told the proprietor they wished to see the surrounding scenery. It was then arranged that two members of the store's personnel would accompany the Starr party to spend a day at Manitou Springs.

The four men stopped at the Spaulding House to pick up Mrs. Jackson, who in reality was Henry Starr's wife. The party spent the day at the springs and then returned to their hotel late that night. Henry Starr and his wife went to their room, while Wilson took the horses to the stable. Learning from the hotel manager that the supper hour had long passed, Henry Starr and his wife went to the Royal Cafe to dine. Just as he began to eat, several officers entered the cafe and placed Starr under arrest. He submitted to arrest peacefully, firmly believing that the officers had mistaken him for someone else.

"Who do you think you arrested?" Starr inquired at the jail.

"Henry Starr, bank robber," one of the officers replied.

Seeing that denial was useless, Starr admitted his identity and that of his wife. The same night Wilson was shadowed to a bawdy house, where he was arrested by officers who forced their way into the building.

A thorough search for the money stolen at Bentonville was made at the hotel room. Under the pillow they found $1,460 in currency and $500 in gold coin. When asked her maiden name, Mrs. Starr said she was the daughter of the Jones family; that she came from Joplin, Missouri and was eighteen years old.

The Federal authorities at Fort Smith sent Deputy United States Marshal William Smith to Colorado Springs to return the prisoners to Arkansas for trial. The two robbers were indicted jointly — Starr for the murder of Floyd Wilson, a deputy marshal who was seeking his arrest a year before: Kid Wilson for his participation in the Bentonville bank robbery.

Henry Starr was convicted of murder and sentenced to die. He appealed his case to the United States Supreme Court, was awarded a new

trial, and in March of 1898 he pleaded guilty to manslaughter. "Hanging Judge" Parker then sentenced him to serve a term of five years in the penitentiary at Columbus, Ohio. In the interim time, Henry Starr had been convicted of three armed robberies, the conviction of which tacked ten more years onto his five year prison term.

Kid Wilson had also been convicted of several robberies and was sentenced to serve twenty-four years in the penitentiary at Brooklyn, New York. Little had been learned of Wilson's family or background. He was once asked about his family or relatives, but he firmly declined giving any information concerning them. All he said was this: "My kinfolks have never done anything to place me where I am; they live on the other side of the globe and I prefer to say nothing of them."

Henry Starr was a half-breed Cherokee Indian, the son of Hopp Starr, who died in 1888. Hopp was the son of Tom Starr, a vicious Cherokee, but most of the Cherokee Nation Starrs were excellent people. Henry was five feet nine and one-half inches tall, had black eyes and hair, and for the most part was good looking, beardless face young man. At the time of his arrest he was twenty years old, while his accomplice Kid Wilson was twenty-five years of age. Wilson was considered by most people to be the worst outlaw of the two, perhaps mainly because he was older than Henry Starr.

Henry Starr was first arrested in June of 1891 by United States Deputy Marshal Wykoff for whiskey running in the Indian Territory. The grandson of Deputy Wykoff was a close friend of Carl W. Breihan, and imparted some important data concerning Henry Starr to him before Wykoff passed away recently in Davenport, Iowa. In February of 1892 Starr was arrested for horse stealing but was released. In August of the same year he was again arrested for horse stealing and was released on bond. Starr failed to appear at the designated time so the bond was forfeited. His bondsman, Kale Starr and also Henry's cousin, offered a reward for his arrest. It was, therefore, while a fugitive from justice that Henry Starr committed the crime that resulted in his being convicted of murder.

Meanwhile, while still out of prison on bond, Henry Starr had committed several robberies, chiefly the holdup and looting of the express office at Nowata. Express Company Detective J. Dickey rode to Fort Smith, where he secured a deputy marshal's commission for Floyd Wilson, in order that a posse might be formed to hunt for the young outlaw. The possemen proceeded to Nowata, from there going to the ranch of Albert Dodge, where Henry Starr was known to be living at the time. For some reason Starr seemed suspicious of the surroundings that evening, for he did not stop at the house but continued on, riding past the ranch buildings and out of sight. The officers scoured the countryside for several hours but failed to locate the fugitive.

On the following day, while the officers and the Dodge family were having dinner, Henry Starr again rode leisurely past the ranch house. Floyd Wilson dashed from the house and mounted an already saddled horse which Mr. Dodge had just ridden in and raced off in hot pursuit of the outlaw. Starr, just as soon as he discovered the officer in pursuit, stopped his horse and dismounted. Deputy Marshal Wilson did likewise, and there the two men stood face-to-face practically, and in plain view of the house. The two men talked for a few minutes, according to eye-witnesses from the house; then Wilson fired a shot over Starr's head, apparently trying to frighten him into surrendering to him. Henry Starr returned the fire in earnest. An empty cartridge jammed in Wilson's Winchester rifle, and tossing the weapon aside, he endeavored to continue the fight with his revolver. Starr fired several more shots with his rifle and soon Wilson fell to the ground mortally wounded. The witnesses stated that Starr then walked up to the prostrate man and shot him in the chest, holding the muzzle of his pistol so close that the officer's clothing was burned. Starr then calmly mounted his horse and rode away to safety.

The brief but furious fight lasted only a few minutes, allowing the other possemen no time to ride to Wilson's assistance.

This affair placed Henry Starr in the category of a hunted man; his only chance for freedom or for life was to keep from being captured by the officers who now would trail him relentlessly. It was the repetition of the old story which occurred so frequently throughout the Old West.

But the web of Fate weaves in strange ways. In a nearby cell at the Fort Smith prison, where Starr was waiting to be transported to Ohio, was Cherokee Bill Goldsby, a burly Indian-Mexican halfbreed who was scheduled to hang for killing 13 men. On November 8, 1894 Goldsby and his outlaws raided the little town of Lenapah, I.T., about twenty miles from Coffeyville, Kansas. There they robbed the John Schufelt store of its cash contents and several pieces of merchandise that struck Golds-

by's fancy. Parallel with the store, but separated by a vacant lot, was a small cafe. Several paperhangers were at work in the restaurant; heard the shots that the outlaws had fired to frighten the citizens, and peered through the window to see what was happening. One of them, Ernest Melton, was spotted by Goldsby, who resented being watched. He swore an oath, brought his rifle to his shoulder and sent a bullet crashing through Melton's brain.

The police officers learned that Goldsby was seen to visit the home of Isaac Rogers, an ex-deputy marshal, who became a friend of Cherokee Bill, and also that Bill was in love with Maggie Glass, who resided with Rogers. On Tuesday, January 29, 1895 Rogers invited Goldsby to visit them, at the suggestion of United States Marshal Crump, who thought the visit would give Rogers an opportunity to capture the wily outlaw.

Cherokee Bill apparently suspected the real purpose of Rogers' invitation or he had been warned by Maggie Glass. At any rate, he never relaxed his vilgilance or allowed his Winchester rifle to leave his hands. Even that very night, he took it to bed with him and slept in the same bed as did Rogers. Each time Rogers awoke, the outlaw would leap to his feet, threatening rifle ready for instant use.

The capture of Cherokee Bill (Crawford) Goldsby is told by Ike Rogers in his own words, and appeared in contemporary newspapers and court records. It is an interesting bit of history so it is repeated here for the reader.

"I had been instructed by Col. Crump to get him alive, if possible, and I didn't want to kill him but I made up my mind to kill him if I couldn't get him in any other way. Scales and I had our guns hidden where we could get them in a hurry but we didn't want to give him any show to fight. After breakfast, we talked for some time and he began to talk of leaving. He and Scales and I sat in front of the open fireplace. I knowed that we had to make a break pretty soon and I was afraid the girl would take a hand in it when the trouble began, so I gave him a dollar to buy some chickens at a neighbor's, so as to get her out of the way. I also sent my boys away as I had not told them of my plans. Bill finally took a notion that he wanted to smoke and he took some paper and tobacco from his pocket and rolled a cigarette. He had no match, so he stooped over towards the fireplace, to light it, and turned his head away from me for an instant. That was my chance and I took it. There was a fire stick lying on the floor near me and I grabbed it and struck him across the back of the head. I must have hit him hard enough to kill an

— 30 —

ordinary man but it only knocked him down. Scales and I then jumped on him but he let out one yell and got on his feet. My wife grabbed Bill's Winchester and we three tussled on the floor, full twenty minutes. I thought once I would have to kill him, his great strength, and his 180 pounds weight, being almost too much for me and Scales, but finally we got a pair of handcuffs onto him. He pleaded and begged me to kill him or release him. He promised me money and horses, all I wanted. Then he cursed. We put him in a wagon and Scales rode with him and I went on horse back, and started for Nowata. On the way Cherokee broke his handcuffs and grabbed at Scales' gun and Scales had to fall out of the wagon to keep from losing his Winchester, while I kept Cherokee covered with my shotgun. At Nowata, we turned him over to Bill Smith and George Lawson."

Cherokee Bill's case was heard on February 26, 1895, the trial lasting one day; the jury out only a few minutes, returning with a verdict of "guilty". June 25, 1895 was the date set for Bill's execution, but his lawyer, the noted J. Warren Reed, appealed his case to the United States Supreme Court, so the date of the hanging was set aside temporarily.

On July 26th, outside friends of Cherokee Bill smuggled several pistols into his cell by means of tying them to a long pole and passing them through the cell window. Bill later stated that the weapons had been smuggled to him by Ben Howell, a supposed member of the Dalton-Doolin band of outlaws.

On the evening of July 26th Cherokee Bill went wild. He killed Lawrence Keating, one of the night guards, and then holed up in his cell, exchanging shot for shot with a half a dozen prison guards and leaping into the air and gibbling like a turkey every time he fired a shot. Henry Starr finally volunteered to disarm Bill. The guards had no objection; if Starr got killed that would be all right, they felt that he had cheated the gallows anyhow. Henry walked down the prison runway and disappeared into Goldsby's cell. The cubicle buzzed with whispers. Then Starr came back up the runway and handed the guards two pistols. He never told anyone how he calmed the outlaw down, but it is known that both Starr and Goldsby took great pride in the fact that they had Indian blood.

Cherokee Bill was quickly indicted by a grand jury for the murder of Keating. At the trial he was found guilty and sentenced to be hanged March 17, 1896. It might also be noted that the President of the United States denied the appeal from the sentence pronouncing Goldsby to be hanged on March 17th.

Thousands of people arrived to witness the execution of Cherokee Bill, but only a hundred with passes were allowed to enter the walled yard of death. At 2:00 P.M. Bill began his walk from the prison to the gallows, in company of Col. Crump.

"Well, I am ready to go now, most any time. Hell, look at all the people, something must be going to happen. Well, this is as fine a day as any to die."

When asked if he wanted to say anything more, Bill replied, as he stepped onto the gallows: "No, I came here to die, not to make a speech." Then, in a low tone, he added: "Except that I wish the priest would pray for me."

At 2:30 P.M. the final chapter in the life of Crawford Golsby, alias Cherokee Bill, one of the most noted of all Indian Territory desperadoes, was closed when Jailer Eoff sprung the trap that launched the killer into eternity.

A curious note in the life of Cherokee Bill is how the number "13" seemed to plague his actions. Many people believed that Bill had killed 13 persons during his career; the reward offered for his arrest was .$1300; his first sentence was pronounced on April 13th; he killed Guard Keating on July 26th — twice 13 —; he is said to have fired 13 shots during the fracas at the prison; Judge Parker occupied 13 minutes in charging the jury in the Keating case; the trial lasted 13 hours; the jurors and the deputy totaled 13; there were 13 witnesses for the prosecution; many people thought Bill should have been hanged 13 minutes after sentence had been passed; there were 13 steps leading to the gallows, and 13 knots in the hangman's noose! And to add an eerie touch to the number, it took the jury 13 minutes to find Bill guilty — a total of thirteen 13's!

Henry Starr had served a little more than half his prison sentence at Columbus, when President Theodore Roosevelt heard of his heroism in disarming Cherokee Bill at Fort Smith after Keating had been killed. President Roosevelt granted Henry a full pardon and he moved to Tulsa where he started in the real estate business. Later he named his son Roosevelt Starr in honor of the President of the United States.

When Oklahoma became a state, Henry and Mary Starr were among the notables at the inauguration of its firsg governor, Charles N. Haskell. But the minute the Territory was admitted to the Union, the State of Arkansas dug up its old indictment against Henry. They had not forgotten the Bentonville robbery. Henry did not wait around to see if Oklahoma was going to honor the extradition request, but fled and returned to his old art of robbing banks. Strangely enough, it was later learned that Oklahoma refused to grant the request from the Arkansas authorities.

Besides the spare build and features of his ancestors, Henry had also inherited the inherent cunning and woodmanship of the Indian. He used it to his advantage more than once. In the spring of 1908, Henry and two accomplices held up and robbed the bank at Tyro, Kansas, and set off a countryside manhunt. One newspaper account at the time stated:

> Natives all along the way are out with corn knives and shotguns and it would be dangerous for a stranger to pass along the highway after the sun has set. Behind every fence post and every clump of weeds lingers one man or a dozen, ready to shoot down a bank robber or a peaceable citizen without the least provocation.

Henry Starr had one weakness . . . he just loved to hold up banks. He was addicted to bank robbery the way some men are addicted to narcotics. The mere sight of the four letters "BANK" set his wheels clicking and his nerves hopping. It was an obsession with him. He just couldn't pass up an opportunity to step up to the teller's window and sing out: "Hands Up and Hands steady!" Henry did not drink, smoke, nor did he even use coffee or tea; and he had an almost uncanny sense of fair play and honor. His love of gambling was incurable; however, for he couldn't pass up a deck of cards, a dice game or a faro table. His luck was even worse at games of chance than it was at bank robbery. He lost incessantly but never stopped trying. He had a will of iron backed by absolutely no luck. Damon Runyon would probably have called him a determined sucker.

On July 9, 1908 Henry Starr and Kid Wilson held up the bank at Amity, Colorado, now called Holly, Colorado. Amity originally was an unsuccessful attempt by the Salvation Army to colonize this area. On that day the two bandits forced the manager to open the safe, took the money, and subsequently marched the manager and all the witnesses to the crime to a nearby pasture; and made their getaway on horseback. Later, when a friend told him that a posse was on his trail, he found Henry trailing the lawmen.

"I just feel better that way," said Henry. "Long as I got an eye on the sheriff I figure he ain't got one on me."

Leaving Colorado, Starr drifted to Arizona, where he wrote a supposed friend in Oklahoma to send him some money from property he was to dispose of for him. Instead, the man in Oklahoma informed the authorities in Colorado, and Starr was arrested and returned to that state to face trial for the holdup of the Amity bank. He was found guilty and sentenced to the State Penitentiary for a period of seven to twenty-five years. However, he was paroled on Sept. 24, 1913 on his promise that he would never again return to Oklahoma. Henry promised but he liked his home state so much that within several months he was living at 1534 E. Second St., Tulsa. Henry even had the audacity to return to Amity for a time, where he opened a restaurant but the business failed. Apparently Kid Wilson's participation in the Amity affair was his first since his release from prison and his last, insofar as Starr was concerned, for he was never heard from again.

Not all incidents involving Henry Starr were filled with gunplay and stern commands. Sometimes they had their lighter side and were downright humorous. One such instance was the holdup of the Carney State Bank at Carney, Oklahoma on Dec. 29, 1914. Just about 4:00 o'clock that afternoon two men armed with Winchesters and pistols walked up to the bank entrance where several local citizens were seated inside the building, busy whittling willow branches.

"All right, you fellows, mosey on home, we're goin' to rob this bank," Lewis Estes said, waving his Winchester towards them in a menacing manner.

Not much impressed, but fearful the waving rifle might discharge, the men retired to a nearby barbershop. There Estes kept them under guard while Henry tried to rob the bank. One citizen, Herman Stump by name, was giving Starr some trouble. Starr told the rotund fellow, who weighed nearly 300 pounds and was about 5'5" tall, to raise his hands. Stump at once stretched for the ceiling.

"Dammit!" yelled Starr. "Not so high; people will see you from outside."

The two outlaws had a team of horses hitched to a farm wagon, waiting for them at the livery stable, while their getaway mounts were in hiding a short distance from town. Starr took several hundred dollars in silver from the bank and invited the bank clerks to see them off in their wagon.

On the way, the two outlaws would invite everyone they came in contact with to join in the parade. By the time they walked several blocks, more than a dozen men had joined in the jaunt. Herman Stump complained that the walk was getting the better of him. Henry Starr grinned broadly as the stumpy fellow waddled along, hardly being able to keep up.

"Yes, I guess walking is pretty hard on a fat fellow like you," he said. "Here, take this bag of 100 silver dollars for your trouble and keep your mouth shut."

Herman Stump returned the money to the bank, while at the same time Starr and Estes were enjoying supper at the home of Mrs. Horace Page, several miles from Carney.

Max Randall of Nowata told the writers that he recalled one time when some ambitious officers laid a trap to capture the wily Starr. Several men were secreted in a load of hay, while other officers hid nearby on a route Henry was supposed to travel to arrive at this mother's home. However, even though he waited day and night, Randall stated nothing happened, for Henry had circled the town and had entered from the opposite direction from the spot where the trap was to be sprung. Henry also stayed with his mother that night, unmolested.

Henry Starr did not rob banks all his life. He worked at one time on the Half Circle Box Ranch, owned by J.S. Todd, in Rogers County, south of Nowata. In the 1890's he worked on the Arthur Dodge ranch on California Creek, northwest of Nowata. This was the XU Ranch. He was working there when he is supposed to have robbed two banks in one day, one near Tulsa, Okla. and one in Arkansas. He left the ranch one evening and the Oklahoma bank was robbed early the next day . . . over 50 miles from home. Later the same day the Arkansas bank was robbed. Henry returned to the ranch the following morning after traveling about 200 miles in two nights and one day. When told that he was suspected of being the robber, Henry simply said, "It would be impossible unless the man was riding an XU horse."

Friday, March 26, 1915 dawned bright and clear, with Marshal Ward Lycan of Stroud, Oklahoma busy cleaning his little office. His office boasted a telephone for emergency calls; something that the old time lawmen did not have. Suddenly the phone range. An excited voice on the other end informed the marshal that a band of seven men, heavily armed, was camped about two miles east of the town. The caller also informed the lawman that the men were doing extensive target shooting.

"Probably hunters," said Marshal Lycan to the caller. "We have a lot of them in Creek County nowadays." With that he hung up and paid little attention to the matter.

Next morning at 10:00 o'clock these same seven men rode into Stroud. They rode in singly and in pairs so as to avoid suspicion. Shortly thereafter, they met at the stockyards, where they left one man in charge of the horses, the remainder of the party splitting up into two groups.

Henry Starr took two men and went to the Stroud National Bank, while Lewis Estes led the remaining men to the First National Bank. All did not go well with Starr as he entered the bank building. There he was recognized by Lee Patrick, president of the bank, who had done business with Henry at his Skiatook bank.

"Put all the money laying around in this sack," ordered Starr. "Then open the safe and be quick about it."

Patrick explained that the safe had been opened several hours earlier and that at the present time the time lock had been turned on.

Starr leveled his gun at Patrick's head. It was evident that the outlaw was angry with Patrick's refusal to open the safe.

"I'll kill you if you don't!" cried Starr. "And you'll be the first man I killed in a robbery."

As the revolver hammer clicked back, Lorene Hughes, a six year old girl, walked into the bank.

Fearing that the child might be injured, Starr suddenly forgot all about Patrick and lifted her to a chair. As Starr handed the little girl a handful of pennies, he said, "Here, honey, play with these and be a good girl, and I will buy you some ice cream when I come back."

Starr then turned his attention back to the robbery. He forced the bank officials to walk as body guards for himself and his men. They were marched down an alley, and then up the street to the First National Bank. In this bank Estes and his men covered the bank people and the customers with their weapons, and demanded their money.

The cashier, H. E. Breeding, removed $4,200 in gold, silver and currency from the vault and handed it to the robbers. He saved $2,000 by tossing it under the safe while he was removing the other money. O. E. Grecian was forced to pick up a number of silver dollars which had been dropped to the floor, while the outlaws waited for Starr to join them.

By now the town of Stroud was in a turmoil, and every able-bodied man was searching for a gun, and stationing himself around the bank. As Starr and Estes marched the bank officials and customers toward the stockyards, they were covered by many guns from many vantage points, but the fear of bullets hitting the hostages inspired caution on the part of the townspeople. A few isolated exchanges of gunfire took place, but no one was wounded.

Henry Starr had accomplished what no other outlaw in history had ever done . . . successfully robbed two banks in the same town at the same time. But his success, if that it can be called, was short-lived.

Paul Curry, a nineteen year old son of a grocer, searched for a gun in vain. Finally he grabbed a short-barreled rifle used by a butcher to kill hogs, saying, "If you are not going to use that gun, give it to someone who will use it!"

Running through a store building, Curry found himself opposite Henry Starr. He shot and Henry fell with a wound in the hip. The loss of their leader did not deter the flight of the rest of the outlaws, for they raced through the town at break-neck speed. Curry aimed at Estes, who had not yet mounted, and shot him in the neck. Estes forced two of the hostages to carry him until they reached their horses at the stockyards.

The outlaws rode to the south of town, with everyone with a gun shooting after them, and even being pursued by an automobile. Estes was found deserted about two miles to the south, and the others were captured two days later.

Back in Stroud, young Curry was standing over Starr.

"Throw away your gun or I'll kill you!" cried the youth.

"I'm a bank robber and I've been caught," Starr told the sheriff. "That's all there is to it."

Starr and Estes were taken to the county jail at Chandler, where a rumor of a lynch mob was spreading, but nothing materialized.

Henry Starr received a sentence of twenty-five years after pleading guilty to the robbery. At the State Prison Henry Starr turned on all his personal charm again. In a few years he convinced the attorney who had prosecuted him, the judge at the trial, the jurors, and the governor that he was really going to turn over the proverbial leaf this time for sure. In 1919 he was paroled again.

For Henry the end came in February of 1921, at Harrison, Arkansas. It was a crisp winter morning that February 18th when Henry Starr and his men strolled into the Peoples National Bank at 10:00 o'clock.

"Hands up and hands steady!" The command resounded through the bank building like a peal of doom. Everyone in the bank threw his hands high except the president, William J. Myers. Myers was a shrewd banker. His bank had never been robbed,

even during a virtual epidemic of robberies a few months earlier. Yet he hadn't overlooked such a possibility, and twelve years before that February morning he had built a back door in the vault, opening into his office. While his customers were being scared to death and the outlaws were busy rounding up all the loose cash in the place, Myers slipped inside the vault. As an added precaution, he had stashed a loaded rifle inside.

In all previous accounts the weapon used by Wm. J. Myers is referred to as a shotgun. However, recent research into the matter reveals this weapon was a Winchester 1873, .38 Caliber rifle, and presently is the property of Wm. J. Myers, son of the man whose shot killed Henry Starr.

Stealthily Mr. Myers took up his rifle and crept to the front of the vault and slowly pushed open the door. Henry was busy stuffing money into a canvas bag. The bank president took careful aim at the outlaw and fired. The bullet ripped through Starr's spine, and he fell to the floor, writhing in agony. The rest of the outlaws went berserk. None of them could tell where the shot had come from. One of the bandits leveled his pistol at the head of the bank cashier, Cleve Coffman.

"Don't shoot him!" cried Starr. "Just get out of here, the lot of you."

"I don't blame you at all," unlucky Henry told Myers. "I would have done the same thing if I had been in your place."

In his final days Henry Starr asked to see young Coffman. The youthful cashier stayed at the dying's outlaw's side for three days, trying his best to console him. Now Henry was alone, even his wife had divorced him the year before, claiming desertion and non-support. Before the end came, Henry presented Coffman with his .45 calibre Colt's Army model revolver.

"Use it wisely, son; I never killed a man during the course of a robbery. I always tried to conduct my affairs, no matter what they were, in the whitest manner possible."

Starr continued . . . "once a fellow falls, it is hard to rise again. All young men should know that crime is a losing game, no matter who the players may be. I wouldn't take 17 million dollars to endure over the agony I have already endured."

On February 22, 1921 Henry Starr died. He was buried February 25th at Dewey, Oklahoma, near the grave of his son. Penniless and un-mourned, the only thing Henry Starr had left was his grave . . . paid for to a Tulsa undertaker years before by the outlaw.

An analytical study of Starr's career results in

the conclusion that he simply could not resist the lure of the outlaw life. He knew that it was to his interest to remain honest, but the call pushed him on. Much of Starr's waywardness and trouble was due to his close friendship for Kid Wilson, a confirmed criminal. The two knew each other as boys, and rode the long, lonely trail together for some years. A careful study reveals that most outlaws of the southwest who attempted reformation succumbed to those earlier associations.

If there are any discrepencies in Henry Starr's story and statements made in the introduction, dates or proper names, it must be remembered that Starr was an occupant of the Colorado State Penitentiary when he wrote his little book. He did not have access to the court records as did the authors.

In all, this is a well-written and most interesting little book about this outlaw's life and his many lawless acts. The text is hereby given exactly as it appears in the original; with stretches of misplaced text and spelling errors. The author ends his book with a bitter tirade against society, and gives his opinion and comments relative to the graft carried on in Judge Parker's Court.

* * * * * * *

Henry Starr, wife and child.

(Top row) All Henry Starr. Left, as adult; center, as boy in very rare photo; right, as he entered Colorado State Prison. Henry Starr in jail. (Photo courtesy R. L. Mach Collection of Western Outlaws).

(Opposite bottom) Colorado State Prison, built 1869.

(Right) Rare photo from tintype of "Poker Alice" Tubbs, famous woman gambler of the Old West who often operated in the Indian Nations.

(Above) W. J. Myers, president People's National Bank, Harrison, Ark., who shot Henry Starr in robbery attempt. (Above right) Friend of Henry Starr, Annie McDougal, known as "Cattle Annie", notorious woman bandit of old Indian Territory. She was said to "peddle whiskey to the Indians, steal horses and cattle." In 1894 she was sentenced to Federal Reformatory at Framingham, Mass. (Below) Winchester 1873 .38 cal. rifle Myers used to shoot Starr.

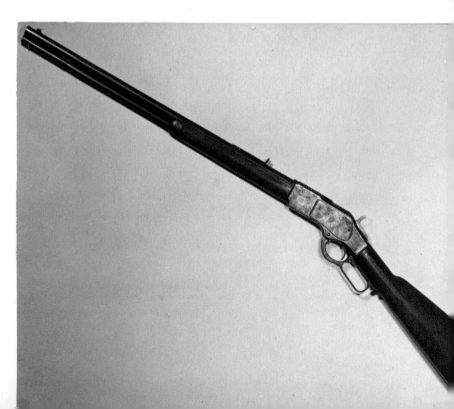

(Right) Lee Pollock of Vinita, Oklahoma, who as deputy sheriff arrested Henry Starr at one time.

(Below) Moving picture actor Tom Mix talking of the Coffeyville bank raid in October, 1892, with the sole survivor of it — Emmett Dalton. His path and Henry Starr's crossed many times.

Two Kansas towns that figured in the embattled careers of Bella and Henry Starr — above, Hays, and below, Caldwell.

(Above left) "Black Jack" Christian, outlaw of Indian Territory and Oklahoma Territory, later notorious bandit and stage robber of New Mexico and Arizona. (Above right) Heck Thomas. (Below) Outlaws killed in Coffeyville, Kansas, raid, 1892 — left to right; Bill Powers, Bob Dalton, Grat Dalton, Dick Broadwell.

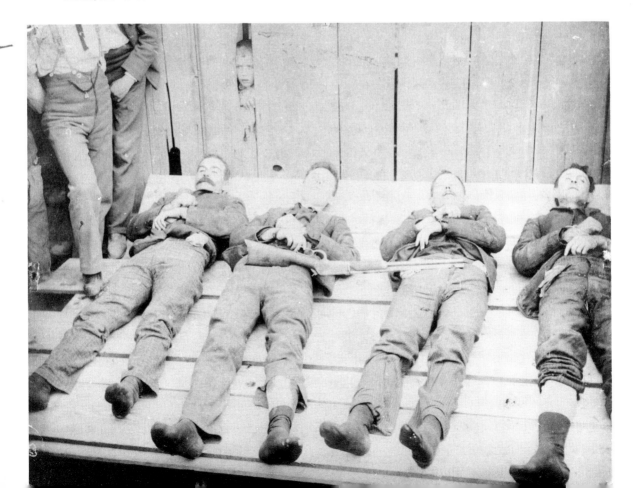

Small headstone is Henry Starr's in Dewey, Oklahoma, cemetery.

THRILLING EVENTS

LIFE OF
HENRY STARR

Famous Cherokee Indian Outlaw
Narrates His Many Adventures
from Boyhood to Date. : : :

WRITTEN IN THE COLORADO PENITENTIARY BY HIMSELF

PUBLISHED JULY, 1914, AND SOLD BY R. D. GORDON, TULSA, OKLA.   PRICE 50c

40

HENRY STARR—HIS BOOK.

I was born near Fort Gibson, I. T., on December 2, 1873, and am of Scotch-Irish-Indian ancestry. My father, George Starr, was a half-blood Cherokee Indian; my mother, Mary Scott, is one-quarter Cherokee. There were three children by their union—Elizabeth, the eldest, Addie, the second, and myself, Henry George Starr, the youngest. I might mention that I was born in a cabin, the inevitable log-cabin, close to Fort Gibson, one of the oldest Forts in the West. It was here Sam Houston came when he fled from his beautiful wife and the governorship of Tennessee, and later married the fair Indian maiden, Talihina. Sam Houston was also famous for his ability to put much "fire-water" under his belt, and his accomplishments along that line were the envy of every Indian and soldier in that region.

Washington Irving also visited Fort Gibson, and it was while ruminating along the banks of the beautiful Grand River, that he wrote "The Bee-Hunt" and other stories.

James G. Blaine, he of the "plumed-knight" fame, after being so ingloriously unhorsed by fisherman Cleveland, sought to forget the sting of defeat by visiting the frontier, and stayed a long time at Fort Gibson as the guest of an army officer.

I spent my boyhood like thousands of other American boys. At the age of eight, I started to school, a distance of four miles, and I always made the trips to and from school on horseback. My teacher was a Scotchman from Canada—a highly educated and polished gentleman, but possessed of a most violent temper. All of the pupils were Indians and four-fifths of them of mixed blood. I went to school to this bullet-headed Highlander for two and a half years, and am proud to say that I held my own with all comers in class-work. At the age of eleven I was in what I should judge would be the sixth grade; that ended my schooling. My father's ill-health made it necessary for me to stay at home and I can honestly say that it was with regret that I gave up my books to help win our daily bread. It was decided that I should try my hand at farming, so I hitched two horses to a ten-inch plow and literally dug into our farm. Critical neighbors said I couldn't plow; my sisters said I was too small to plow. This comment got under my

1

skin and I made up my mind that I would not only prove to them that I could plow, but that I could also raise a crop of corn. My furrows were neither sraight nor regular, but, barring whacks in my ribs and stomach, received from the plow-handles, I got my field plowed O. K., and with only a few days' help from a neighbor at critical periods, I really raised a splendid crop of corn.

This strenuous work taught me patience and self-reliance, and a stick-to-itiveness that has been of great value to me all my life.

The Cherokee Nation, up to the year 1904, elected a Chief, second Chief, Senate, Council, Judges, Clerks and Sheriffs by popular vote every four years. There was a penitentiary at Tahlequah, the capital. The convicts wore stripes, and as a child, the sight of them filled me with terror. There was also an Orphans' Home and a public school in all neighborhoods where there were ten or more children. In the early days there was no provision made for the education of white children in the Indian Territory. The tolerant Indian school directors allowed the white children to attend free. Since statehood, hundreds of full-blood Indians have quit attending school because they are taunted and insulted about their nationality. The teachers were afraid to take the part of the little red children lest the white parents become miffed. The scandal becace so widespread that the Federal government took cognizance of conditions. White men could not vote or hold office, or be arraigned in court for any offense whatever against the life or property of an Indian citizen.

In 1886 my father died, and few months later my mother married a man named C. N. Walker of Arkansas and Texas, a sallow, malarial, green-eyed reprobate who rented an adjoining farm. He was a greedy rascal who saw a fine chance for exploitation of rich lands, with free range and no taxes. There may be a few good step-parents (I have seen a few myself) but I hold it does not pay to examine a snake's tail to see if it has rattlers. I had always looked upon the Indian as supreme, a: the white renters as poor white trash who moved from year to year in covered wagons with many dogs and tow-headed kids peeping out from behind every wagon-bow, and who, at the very best, made only a starving crop. In the days of my childhood the Indian landowner was

2

looked up to by his white renters, and always treated with courtesy and respect; but the years have brought about a great change; the white man holds power, and the same hypocritical renter has grown arrogant and insulting; whenever the Indian is spoken to at all, it is with a sneer. The Indian, and especially the fullblood in Oklahoma, is an outcast in his own country, and it is with a feeling of sadness and apprehension that I think of his future. Broken treaties, misplaced confidence and insult have made him lose interest in life. I have more white blood than Indian, and with my knowledge of both races, I fervently wish that every drop in my veins was RED. I admit that the white race is the superior, but oh, the price he pays for his superiority!

From the first I seemed to be able to read my step-father like an open book, and we were secret, if not avowed enemies. He lost no opportunity to slip one over on me by exaggerating to my mother my most trivial misdemeanors, and was forever complaining of my utter worthlessness and meanness. I confess I was sullen and inclined to "talk back," and if he asked me to do any work I complied with poor grace. Why should I work for this scheming renegade, when I KNEW he would take everything away from my mother, which he later did? It had always been the custom at home to allow the children to claim horses and cattle. I owned a saddle pony and saddle, independent of anyone, having earned the money to buy them. He and I got along without an open rupture for about six months, but one morning he told my mother a deliberate lie about some trivial thing I should have done, and I very promptly said it was a lie. Such a thing was les majesty, in the opinion of my mother, and a look from C. N. was a sufficient cue. She ordered me from the table, saying she proposed to give me a licking that I should remember. I replied that I intended to finish my breakfast; then if she and C. N. wished to try to whip me, they could. I had always stood for her switchings as a matter of fact, but I did not intend that anyone should lick me over a lying stepfather. So when she came to begin operations I firmly pushed her aside. She called C. N. and the hired man to hold me, and by this time I was so angry that I told them I would certainly kill them if they laid hands on me. Of course, they could have easily overpowered me, but if they had, the stepfather question would have been settled for all time. Of course, this incident made things harder for me at home, and a few days later I ran away from home on a pretense of going hunting. I first went to a dance a few miles south, then to my father's sister's, where my sister and her husband also lived. They were glad to give me a home, and so I went to work for them. About a month later my mother came after me, and I told her I didn't intend to go back; she was very angry at my refusal and tried to whip me. My sister and her husband told her that I was getting too big to be whipped, and as I was satisfied with my work, why not let me stay with them. They knew my home life had become unbearable since the advent of C. N., and shared my dislike for him. So mother took my horse and saddle and went home. A few weeks later my uncle by marriage came to see me, and urged me to go back. Knowing that this uncle was my father's best friend, I listened to him. I still think his advice was bad, and can also see the fine Italian hand of my stepfather—the craven was afraid of criticism if I stayed away, and had begged my uncle to persuade me to come home. I returned with the understanding that no one would every try to flog me. In January, 1888, we moved from the old home to the northern part of Indian Territory, and about twenty miles south of Coffeyville, Kansas. Before leaving, my stepfather showed his petty, grasping nature by selling my pony and saddle. The new country filled me with high hopes—miles and miles of prairie, where one could ride unhampered by high fences and timber. I aspired to own cattle and horses to graze on this fine range, and in the spring I began planting corn at 50 cents per day.

My stepfather had two grown brothers and a couple of sisters living near, and I must say that these two boys were as fine and honorable fellows as I ever met, and they both knew what sort of a fellow my stepfather was. Each of them had numerous chances to betray me in after years, when large rewards were offered for me, dead or alive, but they wern't that kind. And at this writing I hold the friendliest feelings for the entire family, excepting C. N. I cannot perceive how prothers could be so different. Through Jeff, the oldest of the two boys, I got a job on the   (half-circle-box) ranch in the fall of '81. My boss was James S. Todd, an old Texas cowman, and one of the finest I ever worked for. He was well educated and possessed of plenty of common sense, and I believe, even now, he will testify that I was always on the job. His present home is in Fort Worth, Texas.

Guess I would be working for him yet and all the things of the past averted if it hadn't been for the following incident: One morning before breakfast, and just as I returned from wrangling horses, I happened to be riding the favorite horse of the man we were boarding with. I met Todd as I rode into the yard, and he said that a large number of cattle were about to cross the backwater of a creek, and for me to hurry as fast as I could and throw them back, as about a hundred had already swam over. Now, I had always been anxious to serve Mr. Todd to the best of my ability, so I forgot that I was on the favorite horse of another man, and rode him at a clip to make the sweat and lather come in profusion; about an hour later his owner arrived, and when he saw his pet all but out, he was wild with rage. I told him of the boss' order to throw the cattle back without delay, and that I intended to do it if it killed every horse on the ranch. We had some words, and when I got back to the ranch I informed Mr. Todd that I intended to quit, and why. He told me I could work on if I wished; that the other fellow and his horse were working for him and for wages, just the same as I. But the bee was in my bonnet and I quit. You don't find many as square as James S. Todd.

I was idle only a few days. I got a job close by, herding some fine beef steers, and after shipping I visited my kinfolks back at the old home, going a distance of a hundred miles on horseback. This was in the fall of '90, and I had blossomed into a man, weighed 144 pounds and was very proud of the fact. This same fall I began work for the   (open A) people, a small Nester outfit with a ranch near Mr. Todd's. They bought cattle wherever they could, and from one head up. This work lasted until the first of the year '91. Then I secured work with a Mr. Roberts, who had a small outfit in the same locality. I had not been fired by the Open A people; their cattle had all been shipped and there was nothing to do. I rode for them again the following year.

While working for the Roberts boys, two strange horses drifted into a pocket formed by two farms and a pasture joining them (Diag.). As there was no water in this pocket, it was plain that they were runaways. The boys said for the first one who rode that way to let them into the gate to water, as no doubt some one would be on the hunt for them soon. I let them in and, noticing that one of them bore saddle marks, I rode him several times. I also informed other ranchers that he was a stray. In something like a month, Charles Eaton, his owner, came after him, and seemed pleased to find him in such good condition, even offering to pay me for my trouble. This was in October, '91, and in December, same year, while I was in Nowata, a small railroad town near the ranch, a vicious-looking fellow, who said he was a Deputy United States Marshal, read a writ charging me with the larceny of Eaton's horse. I was too badly scared to be indignant over such a fake charge, as I knew nothing about laws, courts or justice. The warrant had been sworn out by Charles Eaton, the same fellow that had been so profuse in his thanks for the care I took of his horse, and that simply stunned me, nor do I know to this day what made him prefer the charge, as he swore the truth later. I asked to send word to my friends, but was refused. I was taken to a hotel and handcuffed and placed in a room, the loathsome Eaton acting as guard. For supper they gave me a hunk of sausage and some crackers, and that night I was chained to the bed as though I were the foulest murderer. Even now, murder gets in my blood when I recall the cold chains on my innocent limbs. My faith in the majesty of the law and in my fellow man weakened, and during those long hours on my way to Fort Smith I was still handcuffed. The marshal told me that a certain attorney there might be able to get me out of this trouble, and as I was inexperienced, I took the bait. Hence, on our arrival I was conducted to the office of this legal vulture and gave him $22.00, all the money I had, and a bill of sale for my horse and saddle. Shame upon the fair name of our government for being a party to such a condition of affairs; instead of giving that protection pledged in sacred treaty to the Cherokee Indians, here was a commissioned officer of our government conspiring with a contemptible lawyer to cheat an innocent Indian boy out of a few hard-earned dollars. I shall not honor this lawyer by giving his name; he is only one of many of that stripe who disgraced that bloody and corrupt Federal Court at Fort Smith, Ark.

6

From the attorney's to the jail I was not accused of being faint-hearted, but the sight of that old structure and the rough attitude of the officials chilled my heart. I could also hear the yells and the curses of the 200 prisoners, who were allowed to scream as loud and as long as they desired. I was put on the second floor, the location for horsethieves and highwaymen, and no sooner was I thrust through the door than a bleached-out prisoner let out a series of yells and cries at me of "Fresh Fish!" whereupon the rest began to taunt me and laugh. I was hustled down to the "angaroo Court" by this sheriff and a deputy, the sheriff all the time bawling, "Oh, yes, the Honorable Kangaroo Court is now in session." This business was all Greek to me. The judge fined me fifty cents for breaking into jail without consent of the inmates. Of course, I didn't have a cent, and the sheriff knew it. The bleached-out heavy one noticed a light gold ring on my finger, and made a grab at it, saying that the "Court" would keep it for security. The ring had been loaned to me by my sweetheart, and to have that foul old jailbird even touch it was a desecration. I forgot that I was in jail or court, and smashed him on the nose and the sheriff on the chin, and we went at it for keeps. It was soon evident to his friends that he was overmatched, and they started to help him. At that minute a big, full-blooded Creek Indian came up and kept everybody off while I put the finishing touches to my man, and I certainly made him let out the big squeak. I was not tired nor hurt, and expressed my willingness to accommodate any of his friends, but they didn't seem at all anxious. Of course, this incident didn't make me at all popular with the sheriff.

The odor of a large, poorly-kept jail is worse than the odor in the animal section of a circus, and this particular jail was the worst ever. I was assigned to a cell, the bedclothes reeking with filth and covered with lice. I sat all night on a small box as far from the bed as I could get, and one never placed in a like position has no right to speculate on my thoughts. I, who had never possessed a cent dishonestly, and who had been taught to respect and revere the law from infancy—that a thief was a low, vicious person, and a jailbird one to be shunned—was put in amongst such men on a charge that I was percetly innocent of, and was degraded and disgraced forever. In the twenty-three years since I have

7

passed through some pretty tough tests, but during the lonely vigils of that night my soul passed through its supreme baptism of fire. I am not ashamed to confess that I wept hot tears—not of fear, but of outraged young manhood. Aside from the trouble I had had with my stepfather, my life had been cleaner than that of the average boy, and I felt that the future could never hold any good thing for me again. My cousin ,Charlie Starr, a prominent cattleman, had heard of my arrest, and had me arraigned the next morning, going on my temporary bond. The lying deputy asked the commissioner for the time to get some more witnesses. Of course, this request was a fake, pure and simple, but it was granted, and I was taken back to that vile cell. During the week that passed most of the good went out of me, and I became a soured, sullen man, brooding over this great wrong that was being done me. As no witnesses appeared, I was brought up for a preliminary hearing. My cousin, Charlie Starr, had seen the commissioner and explained my case. The scoundrel, Eaton, who had sworn out the warrant, knew my cousin would not stand for a crooked swearing, and when he was put on the stand he swore to the truth, namely that he had offered me pay for taking up his horse and caring for him, and was forced to admit that there was a doubt in his mind that I had attempted to steal his property. Mr. Eaton was the only witness on his side, and I was promptly discharged. The commissioner gave Mr. Eaton and the deputy a severe reprimand in open court, but I can see now that this was only horseplay to appease the just wrath of my uncle. He should have had Eaton arrested for perjury and taken the deputy's commission away from him. I should have been given a hearing before being put in jail, and the reason I wasn't was because the deputy got $125.00 for committing me to jail; he also got something like $40.00 for mileage, 50 cents for the sausage and 50 cents each for the breakfasts I was supposed to get, but didn't. Eaton received over $20.00 for mileage and $1.50 per day while waiting for the trial, making a total of between $95.00 and $100.00 that the government was out. (Every word can be corroborated by records at Fort Smith.) A good investment for the making of outlaws. This ended my first introduction to Fort Smith's famous and infamous court. Later I shall have more to say about it, as I have only scratched the surface in the telling of the foregoing.

I returned to Nowata with a sad heart. I was lowered and cheapened in my own estimation; to have been arrested for horse-stealing was something dreadful, and I was not able to appreciate that being discharged removed the reflection from my character. I was ashamed to visit my sweet heart, but the sly miss came to where I was staying, and with true woman's intuition, brought up the subject. She told me that everybody who knew me knew I was innocent, and invited be over to see her the following Sunday.

Am I a child of misfortune, or is it just plain "damn bad luck"? Privately, I don't believe completely in anything that has or ever will happen; only in the inexorable law of total obliteration and nothingness.

I again began to work on the Open A ranch. On my way to the Delaware Indian payment a few miles distant, I passed through Nowata. A man I had known for tour or five years asked me to take his grip over to the payment grounds. He had come over horseback and I was in a buggy, and pleased to be of any slight service to him, so I put the grip in and started for the grounds. About two miles out two Deputy United States Marshals overtook me and commanded me with drawn guns that I get down out of the buggy and allow them to search it. I readily complied, and to my surprise and consternation, the grip contained two pints of whiskey. I told them that I had no knowledge of the grip's contents, also that I did not drink. "So," said one of them, "then you must have intended to sell it, and that makes the charge against you more serious."

It was a penitentiary offense at that time to sell liquor in the Indian Territory. I did not inform on the owner of the grip, for I was satisfied that it would not help me. I knew that those scheming officers were stuck to make fees out of my bad luck. My previous experience with the law had taught me the instability of justice. A United States court covering whiskey and misdemeanors had been established in Muskogee, Indian Territory the year before, and they took me there. That night, for the second time in a few months, I, an innocent man, felt the murder-breeding leg-irons and chains.

The men I was working for immediately signed my bond and took me back to work for them. They knew I was innocent, but advised me to plead guilty, pay a fine and have it over with, instead of fighting a long-

9

drawn-out trial, with no witnesses to help me. When my case was called to trial about two months later, I made a plea of "guilty." One of the Deputy United States Marshals, on being questioned by the judge, had manhood enough to say that he didn't think I was a whiskey peddler, and aside from the former charge of horse-stealing, which had been disproved, my reputation was an excellent one; he didn't believe that I knew anything about the whiskey being in the grip. The judge fined me $100.00, a stiff fine for that offense. I paid the amount and went back to the ranch in debt, and worked hard and faithfully until shipping time.

I was disheartened and disgusted. My respect for the law had taken an awful tumble. I began to think that so long as I had the name of being a "bad one" I might as well have the game. I went to Nowata, a town of 300 people. Everybody there knew me, and beside, I was the champion local footracer. I went over to the depot to see the train come in, and noticed a fat roll of bills in the safe. I became possessed with a desire to make good my bad reputation by robbing that safe. Before the two arrests, each time being perfectly innocent, had I found $100.00, or even $10,000.00, I would have returned it to its owner, but the spirit of retaliation was strong within me, and I was filled with a spirit of injury that made the contemplation of such a deed seem a pleasure. I at once went into the country and told a young man I knew, who was inclined to be tough, that I could show him how to make some money. I had never associated with a fellow that was crooked before, and had a bare speaking acquaintance with this one. He was ready for any old thing, so I told him how easy it would be to hold up the agent at night, as he kept open until 10 P. M., and was always there alone.

Three days later we met by appointment. This was in July of the year '92. As soon as night came we rode out from hiding and like a streak to Nowata—had less than an hour to make ten miles. We hitched in the stockyards and put on our masks, which we had made out of handkerchiefs. Held up the agent and two officials and three loungers with Winchesters and .45 Colts. It was child's play, and as we came out, I fired a few shots, more to let off nervous tension than anything else. We got $400.00.

The night was dark. I was riding a bad horse, and

a few miles out of town my horse bucked into and literally astride a wire fence. I slipped from the saddle and the horse escaped in the darkness. The other fellow had furnished the horse, but the saddle I had borrowed from a party in Nowata, and I knew I would have to find him before morning and get the borrowed saddle, or I would be accused of the robbery. I came back to the location early in the morning and found that the horse had gone to a nearby house, and was cut beyond recovery. The farmer had taken the saddle with him to Nowata and turned it over to the authorities. Of course, the railroad detectives and deputy marshals soon had me under arrest, and off we went again to Fort Smith. This time I did not care, for I was guilty, but I pleaded "not guilty," and my bond was fixed at $2,000.00. It was signed by E. E. Starr, a relative, who was at that time treasurer of the Cherokee Nation, Chief Harris and Mr. Ridge Paschal, Cherokee attorney and politician. I admit I hadn't the least intention of going back to stand trial.

This was in September, and my case was slated for November. I went to stay with my aunt near Fort Gibson, presumably to await trial. About November 5th, or a few days before trial, I went to Nowata. Milo Creekmore, a fellow who had been staying at my aunt's, went with me. My lack of interest in my coming trial caused my friends and relatives to suspect that I intended to scoot to the brush, and they all begged me not to skip my bond. Of course, I said I wasn't going to, but I don't think I convinced them that I was telling the truth. We went to Nowata by train and had only a small sum of money and an old white-handled .45 between us. The weather was cool and crisp and we had no horses or saddles.

A certain old-timer, well known around Nowata, said when I was arrested the first time that all Indians were natural-born thieves, and I MIGHT be guilty of the charge. We were near his house this night, and to keep his opinion of the Indian free from falling flat, I took two of his best horses and the only saddle he had. A few miles further on I took another saddle. I had turned my back on established authority and resolved from that time on to go the limit. We rode several miles and hid our trail and stayed all night at a friend's house. He told me that he had put $300.00 in a store at Lenapah, a

11

small railroad town nearby, and we decided that this was about our size, as we had only one .45 and three cartridges. The next night we rode to Lenapah and took the farmer's hog money. He did not lose it, however, as the store made good his loss. Then we rode about sixty miles into the Osage country and got a friend to buy us each a 38-56 Winchester and new revolvers and plenty of ammunition. I also bought a new Cheyenne saddle from a cowboy. We turned the stolen horses loose and bought others.

The day my case was called at Fort Smith we were in a deep canon far into the Osage country, chuckling at the absurdity of anyone trying to arrest me. A few days later we robbed Carter's country store of $180.00 and drifted south to Fort Gibson. On our way, and a few miles from Wagoner, we stopped at the home of Frank Cheney. It was a cold, sleety night, and we were glad to get shelter. I had never seen Cheney before. He was with me afterward in some pretty snaky places.

The next day near Fort Gibson, Creekmore bought a couple of quarts of whiskey and proceeded to get tanked. I objected and we had some words, and he got on his horse and rode away. The drink business didn't go with me; I had determined to always keep a clear head, so if shooting occurred I could give a good account of myself. I had already settled in my mind that I was not afraid of anybody.

Well, I went back to the vicinity of Nowata, and in less than a month had a fight with Floyd Wilson, a railroad detective, and a former United States marshal. I killed him and made his companion hug the ground so close that he played "'possum." There were six eyewitnesses to this affair, Mr. Arthur Dodge of Granada, Colorado, being one, as it happened on the prairie right in front of his ranch, the "X U," eight miles from Nowata.

The railroad had secured the services of Floyd Wilson, an ex-soldier, and an ex-deputy marshal of Fort Smith, Ark., to hunt me, and they had openly boasted of what they would do to me on sight. The night before the shooting, these fellows had called at my sister's house to see if I was there, had broken down her door and acted in a manner unbecoming to officers and gentlemen. The insults to my sister made me nearly crazy, and their threats to shoot me on sight brought about the killing.

12

I was riding by the "X U" Ranch when they came out and opened fire on me. Every eye-witness to the affair swore that they fired first. Wilson took five shots at me, hitting my clothes twice. I took four at him and every shot went into his body. He died instantly. I then took two shots at the detective and he played dead. I got off my horse to shoot, as I did not want to take chances of his spoiling my aim. My horse ran away, so I mounted Wilson's and leisurely rode away.

I had promised myself never to shoot unless it was to save my own life, and have never had any qualms of conscience over that occurrence. It was simply a case of their lives or mine. They started the fireworks, and beside, it developed at trial that the warrant they held was bogus. They were working for the reward offered by the railroad.

On my way into the Osage county I realized that I had done the one thing I had hoped never to do, and that there was now no turning back. I resolved, that being the case, to shoot as long as I could see gun sights. I scouted through the country, say, in a radius of 60 by 160 miles from the scene of the shooting, and nine-tenths of the people were my friends. They knew I had jumped my bond, was a highwayman and had killed my man, but they also knew of my two previous arrests when innocent, and that I had to kill or get killed in the engagement with Wilson and the other fellow. (Note: Who was the other fellow?) There was a reward of $1,200.00 offered for me, dead or alive, and yet I had scores of friends who would shield me and stand guard over me while I slept; and these men were honest, hard-working citizens, who could easily have shot me while I was asleep and claimed the reward. The majority of these men were white, and I of an alien race. I regard their loyalty as typical of the Anglo-Saxon's sense for fair play, and if I must have white blood in my veins, let it be of that kind. Having known them has made me a better and truer man.

Sometime in January, '93, while stopping at Frank Cheney's, seven miles north of Wagoner, he and I rounded the little town of Choteau on the M. K. & T. Railway. We took everything, including the two general stores and the depot; cleaned up over $400.00. A few days later we paid Inola a visit; cleaned out the general store and depot, securing about $220.00.

13

Frank Cheney was, of course, still posing as a farmer and I never allowed anyone to see me at his place. I was scarcely going around with a chip on my shoulder, but there are still lots of people in Oklahoma who will tell you I wasn't playing the coyote, either.

The two marshals who had arrested me when innocent, took to the tall and uncut. They found out that I was a dead shot, and having "got my man," might remember to their undoing, the large part they had played in making my life a wreck.

During the winter I came near having several encounters with different marshals, two of whom were known as brave men and who had got his man. But whenever danger was close, some good friend was at hand to put me wise to the fact.

They came one day to a house where I was staying; my horse and saddle, which they knew by sight, were in the stable. They stayed a long time. I was waiting for them in the hall at the head of the stairs with my rifle drawn, and could have killed them as easy as shooting two rabbits had I so desired. They went to the stable, where my horse and saddle was evidence of my nearness, but soon mounted their horses and rode away without once looking back. Many years later one of them told me that they both knew I was in the house, but at the time each assured the other that I was not any place around. There are five people living who were at the house that day. I was in no hurry about leaving, for I could tell by their actions that they did not want me very bad. A few days later I was at a friend's home when a marshal rode up, but he went away without learning of my presence.

In February I was going through Verdigris Bottom when I saw two officers coming toward me in a buggy. I slipped off my horse and covered them. They called to me not to shoot, that they were not looking for me. I kept them covered, and they lost no time in getting over the road. The same month I came back from the Creek Country to the Cherokee Nation. It was a winter night, though warm, and there was a dim moon in the west. I had ridden perhaps forty miles and it was about 2:30 in the morning, when I passed through a thick settlement. Every blasted dog in the country seemed to wake and bark. I knew that the barking of the dogs would reveal my course if anyone was out looking, and while I hardly

14

cxpected to find officers out after me, I proceeded with some care. I had friends in that settlement, too, but hadn't been in those parts for several weeks, and knew they would not be looking for me. I came to a point where the road led north; there was a farm to the east and open prairie to the west, the high hills with timber growing down to the road. I dismounted and walked, my Winchester cocked and held in the direction of that timber. The faint moon was casting weird shadows and while not on the watch my thoughts were on higher things. If I had been an imaginative person I could have seen all sorts of hobgoblins and booger-men in the shadows. The spell of the night and the solitude was over me, and I was feeling from the depths of my soul what the poets so weakly express.

I knew there was a lane running east a short way ahead, and I approached it with extreme caution. I hope it will not be considered boasting on my part if I say that for keen sight and hearing I am there with the goods. I had spent most of my life with Indians who were raised in the open, but have failed to find one who could beat me in this respect.

About 100 yards from the lane I led my horse under the shadow of some trees and went forward to reconnoitre. I sensed the approach of someone, and when within about thirty feet of the lane, I saw two mounted men coming from the east. I felt certain they had not seen me, so stepped up to within ten feet of the corner and covered them, at the same time telling them in language more more forceful than polite that I would mow them down if they did not ride straight ahead and not look back. They were scared to death, and as they rode away like two statues into the night, I taunted them with the fact I was Henry Starr, bandit and dead-shot, and why not come back and get me and the $1,200.00 reward on my head. Had the situation been reversed, they would have sent me to the boneyard. I rode about a half-mile to the east, and as I came to creek-bed without any timber, I noticed three men riding out of a gully not sixty yards away. I was off in a jiffy and fell flat on the ground; they, too, dismounted and stood behind their horses. I saw their Winchesters glisten in the moonlight, and why they didn't shoot, or why I didn't, can be answered by the savants. I suppose they, as well as I, dreaded the consequence at such close range. After

15

a few minutes had passed and no word spoken, I knew I had the Indian sign on them. I told them that I was Henry Starr and was ready to fight them to the death; that I had just disarmed their two friends at the head of the lane, and if they didn't back off, I proposed to blow 'em off the prairie. That there is magic in a name, is proved by the fact that they mounted and rode on without having spoken one word. I immediately cut a wire fence and galloped through a wheat field to a friend's house nearby, where I stayed for a few days.

The gossip among the country folk was of great benefit to me. Someone told that I wore a steel breastplate; another that I had shown him the breastplate and places where bullets had hit it. This talk, together with my phenomenal accuracy and swiftness with firearms, made me a truly bogey-man to the best of them. As a matter of fact, I was but an average shot, considering I had handled firearms since I was ten years old. I did make a few scratch shots, however, as the following will show: In January, '93, while at the home of a friend and in the presence of several men, I shot a rabbit dead at 150 yards on the run. The following week I was buying a horse, and three or four neighbors, all friendly to me, were there. I galloped the horse a few yards, saying I proposed to shoot the two top wires on a fence about thirty yards distant. As I wheeled sidewise, I brought my gun up and fired two quick shots; the top and second wires were cut clean about half-way between the posts. I could do the trick about once in three times. I also killed a coyote at 685 measured yards—not flunk— but it was a lucky shot and witnessed by several freinds. Of course, all of this reached the officers' ears with exaggeration common to such stories. One time a party said: "How brave you are!" but I quickly checked him up by saying that an outlaw could not get that high in the scale of courage. The word "brave" should only be applied to those who risk their lives in an honorable calling, such as fighting for their country. Give a man moral courage, and he's got the other fellow whipped; that is, if he believes sincerely in his own cause and holds a clear conscience. A lot of cynical people will smile at the thought of an outlaw having a conscience, but that very thing has given me a brand of courage that has made me entirely free from fear of anything, here or hereafter. You may have heard people say, "He has a brave heart." To my thinking there is no such thing. The proper expression would be: "He has a brave head"—the heart has nothing to do with it, because you first see the object to be feared, and the eye telegraphs the impression to the brain. The brain flashes it to the nervous system, and if the brain gives a false or exaggerated report, cowardice results.

Pardon this digression and I will go back to my story. During that winter I went to a number of country dances. People for miles around had known me since I was a mere child, and I was given a hearty welcome; and while I danced a couple of volunteers would stand guard outside to warn me of any danger. I was like all young men—flattered by the attention shown me by the pretty girls, and never missed a chance to be in their company. For two or three years I had had a Miss May Morrison as a sweetheart, who had grown into a young lady believing the good in me and rejecting the bad. Her parents made no objection to my calling on her still, and the country round, including the marshals, knew I was courting her. Despite the close watch kept for me, I managed to call every week or two. I make mention of her because she played a very important part in my career, as you will see later. She was my first love—I shall not rave over her beauty, as we are always daffy over our first sweetheart, but it might not be amiss to say that she was a beauty, was of Irish-Welsh descent, had auburn hair that curled naturally, large hazel eyes and a fair complexion. I might add that she was as good as she was beautiful.

My friends urged me to leave the Indian Territory, and I decided to get a good sum of money and beat it. So, in March, '93, I broached the subject of robbing a bank to Frank Cheney and found he was willing. I selected Caney, Kansas, a town of two or three thousand, and about two miles over the line, as our field of operation, and we started at once. Frank was riding a fine race mare and I a well-bred horse of speed and some endurance. When we reached the country around Nowata we stopped for a few days' rest and bought two extra horses (common cow ponies) to make our first run on. We left our good horses about twenty miles from Caney and the day before our venture we rode to a friend's house near Caney and spent the night. Of course, we did not tell him of our plans. There were two ladies in the family and we invited a couple of families in to dance. This lasted until 3 A. M., and after a few hours' sleep and a late breakfast, we saddled and started to Caney. (This was on the 25th of March, '93.) Our idea was to ride slow and arrive in town about 3 P. M. We each carried two Winchesters and two revolvers, more than our accustomed amount of arms; but we thought that in such a big venture the extra ones might come in handy. We planned to conceal our rifles about two miles from town and take a chance on doing the work with our two trusty .45 Colts. Felt that we would be able to do the bank and get to the street before the alarm was given; then a few more seconds would bring us to our horses, and if there was any shooting we could give a pretty fair showing with our pistols. Just as we were hiding our rifles, a light shower fell, making the ground a little slippery. I knew the town well and hitched about fifty yards from the bank on a back street. I looked at Frank to see if he showed any signs of "cold feet," but his jaw was set and his blue eyes glowed with determination.

We separated and reached the front of the Caney Valley National Bank at the same time; as we entered Frank stepped to the cashier's window and I to the left. We both drew at the same time. There were several people behind the wicket, and two customers. The cashier ducked into the vault and another official ran toward the back part of the building, I after him; he bolted through a door into the back room, and as he started to close it I thrust the muzzle of my pistol between the door and the sash, and pushed it open. He had his hand on a big Winchester, but I shoved both pistols full-cocked into his face, and he dropped his before I could command him to do so. I brought him and his gun to the front of the bank and stood him in line with the customers. In the meantime Frank had taken a common two-bushel sack from his belt and as he entered the vault he said: "I have kept this sack on my farm for seven years for this very purpose, so here goes."

While he was in the vault I took some gold off the counter, and the paper out of the cashier's drawer. Three customers came in separately. I was watching them and as each entered I put my hat on the counter and as they turned around to shut the door, I poked my gun through the cashier's window and commanded them to come

18

around behind with the others. In a few minutes Frank came out of the vault with his sack two-thirds full of greenbacks; didn't even bother to take the silver. We were confident that there had been no alarm given, but knew these ten or eleven men would certainly do some yelling as soon as we let them go, so we put them all into a high stockade or enclosure of boards about ten feet high in the rear of the bank that we noticed before we came in. There was no opening into the alley and the back door of the bank led into it. After turning the key on them, we made our way to the front. As I stepped out into the street I levelled the confiscated Winchester at a crow on the other side; had no idea of shooting, as most everybody ran to cover. Seeing that they were too scared to try to stop me, I walked down the street to our horses; Frank preceded me and had both horses untied. We lost no time in mounting and rode out of town at half speed. When we reached the outskirts we rode faster and were soon to where our Winchesters were hidden. As we had two apiece, we threw away the one we had brought from the bank, fiirst bending the barrel over a fence. We were only a few miles out of town when several horsemen appeared a short distance behind us. Ahead of us was a hill with some scruboaks on it; as we went over the hill south we turned due east and made a roll big enough to choke seventeen hippopotamus, familiar to me. Our pursuers thought we had made for the Osage hills a few miles southwest and went that way. We got to our relay mount long before night, ate our supper and started southeast, freshly mounted. Just as the dawn appeared, we unsaddled at a friend's house ninety miles from Caney. I was not very tired, so we counted our haul before breakfast. Although the bills made a roll big enough to choke seventeen hippotami, to to our surprise and chagrin, it counted up to only $4,900. The foxy cashier had outmanaged us; we learned afterward that he had thrown all the bills of large denomination (amounting to $16,000.00) behind a pile of ledgers while we were taming the crowd. The bulk had looked so big when Frank brought it out of the safe that I never suspected we had been short-changed by the wily cashier who had tried to run away. Thus ended my first bank robbery.

This bank robbery I was never arrested for, but it is common knowledge that I did it, though I was never indicted; for when arrested, the charge of murder came first. Was afterward convicted on all charges I have referred to.

My reputation as a sure shot and perfectly abstemious man caused a lot of bad men to want to join me, and as the excitement of the game had completely enthralled me by this time, I conceived the idea of recruiting a band of men so desperate that everybody would stand in fear of us. By the last of April I was the recognized leader of as desperate a band of outlaws as ever infested the Indian territory, and that is saying a great deal, as the Indian Territory has harbored some bad men.

We made our headquarters at Frank Cheney's home near Wagoner. The gang consisted of seven, including Frank and myself; we were all spoiling for a fight, and as Frank and I had shown what we could do, the others were anxious for an opportunity to do the same.

I don't think it would be amiss to give a brief description of these men. The names I will give are fictitious:

Frank Cheney, a Texan by birth, but most of his life spent in Colorado, New Mexico and the Territory. About thirty-five years old, fair hair and blue eyes. Daring to the verge of recklessness and a good shot. Possessed of a fair education and somewhat of a wit.

Watt, about thirty-five, sallow complexion, blue eyes, dark hair, well educated, a dead shot and the gamest man I ever knew.

Link Cumpelin, age thirty, well educated, fair hair and eyes; a game man, but somewhat chicken-hearted.

Happy Jack, about twenty-seven years of age, dark hair and eyes; a square fellow and full of sand.

Bud Tyler, thirty years old, very dark and fierce-looking, but a little gun-shy.

Kid Wilson, age nineteen; dark complexion; willing to take a chance, but too hot-headed.

Their finish: Cheney was assassinated in the Indian Territory in 1894. Happy Jack was shot from ambush in the territory in 1893. Watt was killed in a battle with officers in the Territory in 1895. Link died in Alaska in the same year; cause of death uncertain, but it was "natural." Tyler died a natural death in 1908, and Kid Wilson is still supposed to be a fugitive from justice. These statistics go to prove that a lawbreaker has all the odds against him. Few die a natural death or escape the long arm of the law.

To show our contempt for the dinky deputy marshals, we fitted out a chuck and ammunition wagon, and as Tyler was the weakest man at arms, we made him teamster. After leaving Cheney's we camped several days at Pryor Creek. On the 5th or 6th of May, '93, six of us went into Pryor Creek to rob the train. ((Look up Kansas City and St. Louis newspaper files.) Were afterwards convicted of this charge. It took us some time to get the crowd at the depot corralled, but we did and looted everything in sight. We kept the train in siege for an hour. There were two deputy marshals on the train, but the spineless creatures ditched their hardware along with the rest of them. We realized $6,000.00 and a consignment of unset diamonds and no one hurt, although we did a lot of firing as a means of intimidation. After the robbery we rode some twenty miles and established a camp; the country was thickly settled and we did not try to hide. On the second day we were in the vicinity of Nowata and made our way leisurely; had crossed the Missouri Pacific and Frisco railroads several times. We knew that our doings had been telegraphed all over the country, and for sheer hellishness, we decided to give our farmer friends a free daylight exhibition of nerve. We were all superbly mounted on well-bred horses and cowboy saddles. We wore spurs and each man carried aWinchester of large caliber, model eighty-six, and two Colts in fine wide leather belts.

Instead of forming in line like the cavalry, we formed fanshape; each man on the outside was to begin shooting always at the extreme right or left, and the center to center; this was done to keep two or more from firing at the same target. Well, we went through our maneuvers and frightened the whole neighborhood our of their wits. I   don't believe an outlaw camp was ever conducted along the same line as ours. We were shooting at least a hundred bullets a day each to keep in trim, and our expenses per day, NOT including our ammunition and clothes, was $30.00, or $10.00 for each meal. We had every delicacy to be obtained in those days, and always the BEST obtainable. The railroad offered $1,200.00 for me, dead or alive, and the Pryor Creek trainmen $1,000.00, making $2,200.00 for this trick alone. We made no effort to conceal our names; rather, we boasted everywhere we stopped that we could whip all the deputies on the force. These same deputies were willing to arrest innocent and harmless boys and drag them off to jail, and with the fees thus gained drink Fort Smith whiskey and pose as heroes before the demi-monde; but they wouldn't risk their whiskey-soaked and immoral hides in an attempt to arrest real violators of the law, though some of them were regarded as man-killers. I can't recall an instance where a deputy ever killed an outlaw in FAIR COMBAT.

While out reconnoitering with two others of the gang about two weeks after the Pryor Creek affair, my horse went lame. I stopped at a nearby house to get another, but the man living there was newly-married and talked me out of taking one of his. I went a couple of miles further on and asked a red-headed man standing in the yard if he would sell me one of a number that were standing in a pasture a hundred yards away. He said he didn't have any horses to sell to the likes of me, so as we rode by I made my choice of the herd and promptly dropped my rope on him. The man with the red hair did not try to stop me, but walked swiftly toward the house. (Note: This man still lived in the same place two years ago.) I warned the boys to ride up, as the fellow meant mischief. There was a wire gate leading out of the pasture about 350 yards from the house, and just as we reached it, we saw the womenfolk run out of the house to the cellar, and knew the fireworks were about to commence. I jumped from the horse and passed the reins to one of the boys, telling him to keep the horse out of range while I entertained Mr. Redhead. I ran about thirty yards to the right and he sent in the first shot; it passed me a little to the right and high. I took aim at the spot where I saw smoke coming from. I was lying on the ground with an elbow rest, and we exchanged perhaps a dozen shots. His as a rule were well lined, but too high, and he had the best chance to hit, as the two windows and doors gave him a chance to alternate, while mine were all guesswork. Seeing that the horse was out of range, I decided to run for it in a southeasterly course; now a person not familiar with a bullet's flight will ask why I should run southeast. The wind was blowing from the south, which would have a tendency to blow the bullets north and behind me. Another reason is that unless he made allowance for my speed and the distance the bullet had to travel, he

22

couldn't hit me in a year. The standard rifle sends out a bullet at the rate of about 2,000 feet per second; a fellow running at a slow time of 100 yards in fifteen seconds travels at the rate of 25 feet per second, or about ten feet while a bullet is traveling nine hundred or a thousand feet. Hence if a man was running southeast at the rate of fifteen seconds to the 100 yards, and one was to fire a bullet point blank at him the bullet would pass about five feet behind him. My red-headed friend took about six shots at me, but all passed several feet behind me.

On our return to the Cherokee Country we agreed that train robbery was too tame and decided to rob a bank in approved style and shoot up the town while taking the money. This is the old charge that put me on the run this last time. These people found an indictment against me immediately after being taken to Fort Smith, but Uncle Sam had a murder charge and eight or ten cases of highway robbery against me and the state of Arkansas had to wait. Arkansas had the indictment renewed from time to time.

This is the old charge that put me on the run this last time. These people found an indictment against me immediately after being taken to Fort Smith, but Uncle Sam had a murder charge and eight or ten cases of highway robbery against me and the state of Arkansas had to wait. Arkansas had the indictments renewed from time to time.

We selected Bentonville, Arkansas, as our town, it being the county seat and a rich town. It is about twenty miles over the state line. I don't think there can be any harm in telling this affair, for if those Arkansas hillbillies ever get back they will send me to a convict farm for life. We could get within fifteen miles of town and stay hid, but from there it was an open valley thickly settled. We hired a buggy in Bentonville the night before the robbery to transport our rifles across thos farming district without attracting attention. The date was June 5th, '93. At 11:30 P. M., we started, aiming to make the sixteen miles into Bentonville in three hours. Frank and I rode in the buggy and led the horses. The other four rode two and two about a mile apart. As we neared town we closed up and all got to a back street at the same time. We had arranged that Kid Wilson and I were to lift our rifles from the buggy as soon as we dismounted and the other three were to see to the hitching and one stay with the team while the other two covered the ground between the bank and the horses. There were lots of people in town that needed watching. I led the way at a stiff dogtrot, and as the bank door was open, I jumped far into the room from the street, Frank and the Kid at my heels. We gave the usual salutation and proceeded to get the cash. Be had not been in the bank but a few seconds when the shooting commenced across the square; two men from under cover were trying to pepper us with rifles and we returned the fire with vigor, but no results. While Frank was in the vault, poor Link, who was walking back and forth just below the bank, was getting it from all sides. Four or five men were shooting at him—and hitting, too—with shotguns, the shot varying from buckshot to birdshot, and if he came too far up the fellows on the square opened on him. We were in the bank about five minutes and when we came out we brought everybody, the six people who were in the bank, with us, but the shooting was so hot that they scattered in spite of our threats. We had one guy carrying a sack of silver, but he got away. (See files of Kansas City and Arkansas papers of June 6th, '93.) We backed to our horses in good order, leaving three citizens down and dangerously wounded. Link, a mass of shots, one of them in the eyes, was suffering terribly and had to be assisted in mounting. I had our boodle, amounting to $11,500.000, on my arm, and Cheney and I were the last ones to ride out of the valley. We went at a mad pace west toward the Territory. The sheriff, with a large posse, were soon after us, but as there were no telegraph or telephones on our route, he didn't have much chance to harm us. We had ridden perhaps fifteen miles with the sheriff and posse at our heels—not within range, but just dogging our heels—when we passed through a small settlement and told some men to tell the sheriff we were going to ambush them and kill a few of them, and if he escaped and followed us we would get him sure. True to our word, about a mile further on, Frank, Kid and I doubled back on his flank and killed seven of their horses. The sheriff gave up the chase and went on back to Bentonville. We rode part of the night and the next day about 3 P. M., got to Cheney's home. We made no pretense at concealment and rode down main roads, crossed the Grand river near Wagoner at

Ferry, and as Frank's place was on the open prairie, everybody could see us ride up. Link was pretty badly shot, but stuck to his horse like a Spartan; his eye was gone and he could not use his rifle, as he had been shot in the arm. Frank and I decided to take him about seventy-five miles northwest to friends for rest and treatment. We passed within a few miles of Pryor Creek, the place we had trimmed a month before, and a certain party we had stopped over with hastened to Pryor Creek and told that three of us had just left his place and one was badly wounded, and so he could not fight. This was at once telegraphed by citizens to the chief marshal at Fort Smith. He had to make a bluff of some sort, so he ordered out a number of deputies from various points near Pryor Creek to take up our trail and follow us until we were either captured or killed. The people in general regarded this as a joke. We rode only twenty-five miles that evening and stopped at a friend's house on the Verdrigris River for a couple of days' rest; didn't stay at the house, but selected a camp near a deep ravine where three large oak trees grew—a fine place to put up a defense. The next day at 2 o'clock we saw sixteen horsemen a couple of miles away, who were apparently following our trail; we had plenty of time to have made a good getaway, as our horses had rested fourteen hours and theirs were bound to be jaded, but we had the deep ravine, the three big trees and were well-rsted, while the officers had to approach us from the open. We thought the two of us under these conditions would be a match for the whole sixteen, which proves that at least we were at least not much afraid.

They dismounted at our friend's house, got a drink and inquired if he had seen us; our friend told them that he had seen three men riding north early that morning. The marshals knew he was lying, as they had trailed our shod horses in the soft ground to the very door, and also knew we were in the river bottom only a half-mile east; they rode north. Frank and I had each spread a blanket on the ground with about a hundred loose cartridges on them, so that we could grab them quick in case of an attack. It would have been no battle —but slaughter. From our vantage point we could have mowed them down without exposure. In about an hour we heard fifty or sixty shots up the river, but stayed in our location until night. Link accodentally shot himself in the foot about June 20, so we left him at the home of a friend near Lenapah, I. T., and never saw him again, but he got safely away from the authorities.

This brings to my mind the last time that I saw Frank Cheney. He was riding in a flat some distance away. The day was partly cloudy. Just as he reached the edge of some timber, the sun came out bright and his white shirt and the flax mane and tail of his thoroughbred horse flashed in the sunlight. He wheeled to wave me a greeting as he disappeared. I was for a moment overcome with a feeling of inexpressible sadness, as it was understood ever since our return from Bentonville, that I was to quit the country for good, and that noon we saddled horses—I to go west to the Osage Country, and he south to the Creek Country. We had been close friends and both felt the parting, but neither mentioned it that we never expected to see each other again. Our friendship was too genuine for any theatricals or any affectation, so we shook hands quickly. Frank sprang on his horse and headed south and I west. I reached the top of the hill previously described, when Frank turned and waved his last adieu. May his brave soul rest in peace and the traitors that caused his death in eternal damnation.

I went at once to the Osage Country, where I met my friend, Miss Mary Morrison, who lived near Nowata. We had met by appointment and in a covered wagon, with a friend as driver and Kid Wilson as bodyguard, we started for Emporia, Kansas, to take a train for the west, aiming to be married when we reached the coast. In deference to the virtue and memory of Miss Morrison, and to put to route a coterie of gossipers concerning her, that the reason why I didn't marry her while back in Indian Territory, is evident to anyone and I did intend to and would have married her as soon as effectually away. I was betrayed by a party that is now dead. He received $500.00 for information that would lead to my apprehension, dead or alive. We were, no doubt, shadowed from the time we boarded the train at Emporia, Kansas. Our intention was to catch a fast train to California and go from there to Old Mexico. However, we stopped at Colorado Springs to replenish the lady's wardrobe on July 2nd. On Sunday, the 3rd, we were out sight-seeing and did not return until late. I left Miss Morrison in her hotel and went to a nearby hotel to get something to eat, when four plain clothes men jumped on me from behind and other policemen in civilian dress. They did not use any guns, but simply mobbed me—what they term a "roughin'." I learned afterward that they had been looking for a chance to get me all day, but were afraid to tackle me, so long as Wilson and I were together. I was placed in the "holdover," handcuffed. Through treachery of the landlady of a house of illfame, Wilson was arrested shortly afterwards. I admit that this time I was completely whipped without getting in a scratch. If you touch a man's vanity you are sure to touch a tender spot and, of course, I had made up my mind to fight to the end, irrespective of time, location or odds. I had pledged myself that I would not be caught until I had fired my last shot, whether it was on the open prairies of the Indian Territory or the crowded streets of a big city. I, who had made the gun-fighting marshals of the Territories stand back—I the "Bear-Cat" of a bunch of sure bad hombres, had been arrested without a shot being fired, by four or five pot-bellied policemen! I felt utterly crushed and degraded. I was placed ex-communicando and not allowed to consult an attorney. I hadn't committed any crime in Colorado; no one there could swear that I was really Henry Starr. Had I been able to see an attorney not with the gang, I could have got out on a writ long before officers arrived from Arkansas. For two days I was not allowed to buy meals with my own money, but a kind-hearted deputy sheriff at the county jail looked after me and brought in a big drink of brandy and a fine meal and allowed me to go to his office to eat. I didn't drink at all, but gave the deputy the brandy as a bracer to keep his mind off of the fact that he was entertaining so dangerous a man as Henry Starr.

I don't recall my old friend's name, but I remember the kind-hearted deputy as a man of perhaps sixty, with a pleasing smile, long whiskers and a low voice.

As a petty police graft, I mention the following: I was not permitted to spend any money taken from me, but was allowed to pawn a diamond worth $300.00 for $50.00 and when I went back after the diamond later, learned that the ticket given me was a fake. As soon as officers arrived from Fort Smith, Wilson and I were taken to Denver and a few days later to Fort Smith, Arkansas, via Kansas City and Springfield. We were heavily manacled and accompanied by an officer from Fort

Smith and Deputy United States Marshal Brown, from Denver, a fine officer and gentleman. The sensational newspaper correspondents worked overtime. Mine and Wilson's pictures were on the front pages of all the big dailies, but the prize lie of the aggregation ran thus: That the young lady with me was the daughter of a wealthy Eastern family, and that while robbing a train I had been struck with her beauty, and taken her by force to an outlaw retreat, while she in turn had fallen in love with me. As I have already said the lady with me was my "kid" sweetheart then seventeen years old. The St. Louis Republic in particular, printed trash unreadable about her on the front page and the gapings of the crowd all along the line sure made me sore. At Monette, Mo., we were met by Chief Marshall George Crump, a strong force of deputies, and also the sheriff from Benton county, Arkansas, where we had visited with telling results a month before. This weazened faced sheriff made himself obnoxious by asking foolish questions and I finally told him that a man of my reputation and dignity could not afford to hold conversation with a sheriff of a backwoods county in Arkansas. Of course this was horse play to get rid of him but it created a laugh. An immense crowd was at the Fort Smith depot to see us come in. Photographers all along the line and reporters galore were at every vantage point. My attorneys had wired me to make no statements regarding the charges against me. It was July 13—unlucky date—we got to Fort Smith. The newspapers and local sentiment were very strong against me. This is not strange as Floyd Wilson, the man I killed at Nowata, had lived in Fort Smith for years, where he had been a policeman and later a deputy marshal, and his widow still lived there. I had about as much show for justice as a lone sheep in the midst of a pack of gray wolves. I employed as council, the Hon. W. H. H. Clayton, Col. William M. Cravens and Judge Thomas Barnes, all noted criminal lawyers. Messrs. Clayton and Barnes had each served as district attorney for the government at Fort Smith. Despite a hostile feeling and a prejudiced court these men, true to their professional honor fought with a zeal and skill remarkable even in that famous criminal court. The more I learn of the world's hypocrisy and double crossing the more I appreciate the gallant fight these men made for me.

In about forty or fifty days I was brought into court and fourteen indictments were read to me. One for murder and thirteen for highway robbery, as also were Kid Wilson and Alf Chaney, a brother to Frank. We were all convicted. Alf Chaney's conviction is a fair instance of the brand of justice dealt out at Fort Smith in those days. Alf was at the depot at Wagoner, I. T., forty miles south of Pryor Creek, when the train that had been robbed arrived at Wagoner, and proved that fact by a score of reputable witnesses and neighbors who had known him for years. It was also proved by four neighbors that lived in the same yard with him that he had not left the house all the day of the robbery, but in spite of this he was convicted. The only man that swore anything against him was the engineer, who testified that a man who might have been Alf Cheney came by the engine but he really did not see him clearly. The district attorney argued that Alf could have assisted in the beginning of the robbery and then got a freight train into Wagoner ahead of the passenger train. A very weak and absurd contention and in an ordinary court of justice the jury would have acquitted him from the box. That the world may know, I will say that what convicted Alf Cheney was the $1500 reward by the railroad and the express companies for the arrest and conviction of the Pryor Creek robbers. The money was "cut" three ways. Assistant rosecutor McDonough receiving $500; Byers, Chaney's attorney, $500, and Heck Bruner, the marshall who made the arrest, $500. A fat chance a man had with such a bunch when one gets double crossed by his own attorney,—a government official would conspire for $500 to send an innocent man to the penitentiary. The deputy marshal, with his average low order of intelligence and lack of moral courage, was hardly to be blamed.

Alf Craney's lawyer should have had a separate trial for him from Kid Wilson and I, whose reputations were of the worst. As the case proceeded I could see a conspiracy to convict Chaney for the reward, and knowing that I would be convicted, and to save an innocent man, I told his attorney that I would go on the stand and acquit Chaney but my offer was rejected. The cowardly pettifoger was in the scheme to fix poor Chaney and he was given twenty-four years in the pen, ten of which he served. What that poor fellow must have suffered those ten long years is not pleasant to ponder.

If a man or a set of men do wrong, but with honest convictions, they may be censured but still respected, while on the other hand, when a Federal judge and district attorney conspire to deprive an innocent man of his freedom, through the domination of a supine and ignorant jury, then I say down with the law and society, and allow man in his primitive savagery to strike down the man that robs him of his freedom.

I was soon put on trial for the murder of Floyd Wilson. A man is supposed to be tried by a jury of his peers. The proceedings would have been a joke were not a human life at stake. What chance had I, a noted outlaw, of a different race, before a jury in the town where Wilson had lived for years. The evidence was all in my favor and my attorneys felt sure that a verdict of manslaughter would be the severest verdict. The district attorney's argument was based chifely on my reputation. Former Representative Isaac Parker, the judge's instructions to the jury lasted two hours and forty minutes, and for legal pomposity and hazy insinuations, it would rank high. Once he did descend to earth and said that a man like me charged with highway robbery, and one who had also jumped his bond, could not claim the right of self defense. This was a bad break for his high honor, as this was one of the nine errors the case was reversed on by the United States Supreme Court. The jury was out long enough to look respectable and returned a verdict of "Guilty of murder in the first degree," which menat the rope. The judge, to show his appreciation, ordered that the jury be given supper at the government's expense. I had been convicted of the Pryor Creek train robbery before this murder case came up, so was then put on trial for the looting of the depot safe at Nowata. Note the overwhelming testimony of one cheap detective, who swore that I told him I did it—a lie all the way through. Of course I was guilty but the methods these people chose and the ease with which they would convict was something beyond belief. In a few days I was convicted on the two cases of robbing stores. The traitor Creekmore turned state's evidence. If ever a poor devil was a fall guy, it was I about that time. If I was going to hang why spend time and expense convicting me on these highway cases? Of course this exposed the prosecutor's weakness. Kid Wilson and Alf

Chaney were given 24 years at Brooklyn, N. Y. I was not sentenced on the highway charges but was brought in pretty soon and sentcned to the rope. The judge, with his usual ornate vanity, gave me a twenty-minute lecture, but he failed in his object. That fellow never could scare me. He sentenced me twice to the hemp, but I never batted an eye. I was young and foolish in the head in those days. My attorneys promptly took out a writ and this stopped all hanging for me until the United State Supreme Court passed on the case. In about 15 or 16 months my case was reversed and I was remanded for a new trial.

The justice that handed down the decision took occasion to remark that the charge could not be greater than manslaughter. This was a victory for my attorneys and a great rebuke to the prosecution.

Isaac Parker, the Nero of America, was appointed by President Grant shortly after the close of the Civil War, and had jurisdiction over the Western District of Arkansas and all of Indian Territory for a number of years.

During Parker's regime as judge, if a poor devil happened to be sentenced to hang by him and was so bereft of friends and money to take an appeal to the Supreme Court he was hanged within thirty to sixty days after his trial before Parker. Eighty-eight men were hung by Parker's orders and he sentenced a hundred and thirty odd to the same fate and boasted that he wanted to have the "glory" of having had 100 men put to death by his orders.

My case was on docket for the autumn term in the year 1895. July 26, 1895, an attempt was made to break jail by Cherokee Bill, a noted outlaw, under sentence of death. One guard was instantly killed and others were in immediate danger. I pledged myself to get Bill's gun if the guard would give me his word of honor that he would not shoot him when disarmed, which he did. I went at once to Bill's cell and told him that he could not possibly get out,—that he might be able to kill a few more guards, but that would avail nothing, and to take my advice and give his gun to me, which he did, loaded all round. I walked to the end of the corridor and handed the gun to the guards. This is the true account of that affair, and can be corroborated by a number of people still living. A special jury was called, and as a culmination of high-handedness and injustice

I was handcuffed and arraigned with Cherokee Bill for the jail murder. The guards and officials at the jail were furious and indignant, and promised that I should get the best of it. That such dastardly action was bound to react. The low cunning of the Assistant Prosecutor was again shown; no doubt he and the judge had their heads together and smarting under the sting of the Supreme Court's rebuke, decided to play their trump card against me, by having me arraigned with Cherokee Bill, charged with the murder of a jail-guard while attempting to escape, and all in the presence of the petit jury that was to try me for the murder of Wilson. The second trial on the Wilson murder charge was practically the same in regard to evidence as the first. As an illustration of how sure the prosecutor was of his jury, will cite this incident. When the argument of a case is closed it is customary to remand a prisoner to jail; but I was permitted to sit while another case was called. I remarked to my attorney that such proceedings looked bad. In one-half hour the jury returned a verdict of murder in the first degree. The indictment for accessory to killing guard was nolled.

Arkansas is noted for ignorance and Hill-Billyism, and fifty per cent of the jurymen were drawn from backwoods counties and were completely dominated by the powerful personality of Judge Parker, who was no doubt an able man, and of extensive legal learning. But he had fought evil-doers so long that it was claimed by even his most intimate friends that his mind was warped on that particular subject, and those closest to him admitted that he was a Monmoniac on the subject of crime. I can scarcely take so charitable a view of the Judge because he conspired to convict Alf Chaney when the densest mind in the court room could see that he was wholly innocent. And I have personal knowledge of two other cases where rewards were offered for conviction. I do not charge that he got any part of the rewards; on the contrary, I don't think he would have taken money under any condition, but he knew where the money went. I was again sentenced in the fall of '95 and again took the case to the Supreme Court, and granted a hearing about sixteen months later. However, in the meantime, Judge Parker had a newspaper controversy with Justice White of the Supreme Court. Justice White flayed his honor of Fort Smith for flagrant abuse of power, and Parker replied, charging Justice White with a lack of knowledge of the law. Right then Judge Parker got in bad, and for him to say that a Justice of the U. S. Supreme Court knew nothing of the law is a striking example of this man's bigotry and exaggerated ego. I don't pretend to be on the inside, but have a sneaking suspicion that friends of the offended Justice got the ear of Congress and that body promptly and effectivey stripped the Honorable Isaac Parker of his kingly power by taking the Indian Territory from his jurisdiction. They cut off his tail close up,—bully for Congress. I don't care what they do with the tariff. Hurrah for the Supreme Court, the most incorruptable court of the history of the world. Of course the Judge was to dispose of all criminal cases pending, and after that was finished only violators of internal revenue came under his control.

How our good old Uncle Sam got stuck up, shook down, and double crossed by that court at Fort Smith. Court never adjourned,—one term ran on 'til another was due, and let it also be remembered that witnesses came as far as 300 miles and received mileage and $1.50 per day for expenses while at court. A marshal got so much per for each witness subpoenaed, and not one witness out of every four was used, while often 30 or 40 witnesses in one case would remain two months, and then the case would be contiued. If tried, not one witness out of five knew a material fact. Of course we could expect a host of professional witnesses; the same men were called from term to term, stool pigeons of the deputy marshals, haunting the saloons and low dives which flourished and grew fat in Fort Smith. Naturally this swarm of witnesses promoted such industries as saloons and houses of ill-fame, and cheap boarding houses.

It is not my intention or desire to cast the remotest reflections upon the good citizens of Fort Smith; far from it, for during my stay there in durance vile, of four years and six months, I came to know most everybody in town; and I would be an ungrateful wretch indeed if I failed to remember and be thankful for the many kindly favors and expressions of sympathy and cheer proffered by many of the best citizens in the town, who loved fair play, and knew my case was one of 18 karat shanghi. I stayed so long that these good people almost looked upon me as a native son. I wish to add that the guards and keepers treated me with the greatest consideration, and were always willing to do me a favor. I spent most of my time during those long years reading good books supplied by my attorneys and friends. I was eager for knowledge, and was also allowed all and any newspapers and periodicals, and I bought many. I figured that if they did hang me, the information acquired wouldn't make their job any easier, and if they didn't, such knowledge would help me earn an honest living when they released me.

Soon after Congress took the jurisdiction of Indian Territory from Fort Smith, Judge Parker seemed to lose interest in life; the proud head drooped, and soon the gang of fawning syncopants, true to their hyena instincts, sneaked away when they should have stayed to cheer and condole. But such action is as old as history; Kings and Emperors have experienced the same requiescat in pace.

In less than a year Judge Parker was no more. Out of 13 men under conviction of murder with the death penalty, in jail at the time of his death, 4 were acquittetd, 2 given life sentences and 7 found guilty of or plead guilty to man-slaughter. These facts speak more eloquently than words concerning the justice or injustice of the Federal Court at Fort Smith. Hon. John R. Rogers, a former member of Congress from Arkansas, was appointed to fill the place of Judge Parker, and soon disposed of all criminal cases pending. The leading business men of that town saw Fort Smith had a commercial future, and wished the bloody past to be obliterated, and in a speech by Senator Vest of Missouri, on the floor of the senate, he said that the place was a shambles, a butcher's domain, a stench, and a disgrace to civilization and humanity. The old gallows which had for so long been one of the show places of the town and the jail walls, were removed in January, 1898. I came before Judge Rogers for sentence and was given three years for manslaughter, five years for the two train robberies, and four years for the Pryor Creek affair, and one year for the Nowata robbery, making a total of 13 years. Considering the number and gravity of the charges, this was a light sentence. Alf Chaney and Kid Wilson got 24 years for the Pryor Creek affair, and poor Chaney was innocent.

Judge Rogers gave me a kind and fatherly talk, and said if my future conduct was good that the court would in a reasonable time join in a recommendation for a complete pardon. I don't know what the judge thinks of me now, or if his feeling would be a bit kind if he knew some of the facts of my life later; but my sentiment toward him shall always be one of gratitude and the deepest respect.

On January 23, I left Fort Smith for Columbus, O., to begin my sentence, having spent 4 years, 6 months and 10 days in jail. I withstood the sudden change from the sunny South to the cold and frozen North in the dead of winter remarkably well, but many of the poor fellows from the Indian Territory succumbed to the rigorous climate, bad blood, and hard work put upon them. There were over 500 United States prisoners in Columbus at the time I entered. I had my neck bowed to do that sentence and do it well, irrespective of conditions, and my record as a prisoner was perfect; only the rankest of fools and imbiciles give trouble in prison. Hon. E. G. Coffin was warden, and through the intercession of friends granted me many important privileges. I can't think he ever had cause to be sorry for doing so.

My sentence read that no part of it should be spent at hard labor, and my work was peace-meal and easy. I learned the trade of glovemaker and after two years of steady work was considered by outside men who knew, to be compelled to work in any shop. I also worked as assistant butcher, and bread cutter. Since coming to Canon City I have mastered the trade of bread-maker. It is a good trade and I am glad I know it; but I often have been fearful, if the time comes when I am again reunited with my family that my wife will make me do the pastry cooking. Shades of Tecumseh and Sitting Bull! Think of it! The swift and humiliating change,— of an Indian Warrior being forced by a masterful squaw hat awry; he wore a heavy mustache tinged with gray, and there were innumerable wrinkles around the shrewd, kindly blue eyes. He wore blue overalls and top boots, and a flannel shirt open at the throat; as fine a type of manhood as I ever have seen in my life, and worthy of the painter's best efforts. "Fall off, boys," said he of the boots and funny white hat, and as we dismounted, he walked to the kitchen door and bellowed: "Two more for breakfast, mother, and hungry ones, too, if I'm

35

a judge." While stabling our horses, I learned that he had settled on this farm the day of the big opening, April 22, '89, and had also been on the place long before the opening; he showed us the dugout he had lived in when the United States soldiers moved in beyond the Kansas border, but on the opening day he was first in the rush, and got the very land he had so long wanted. I congratulated him on his staying qualities, and that it paid is proven by the fact that he now owns 320 highly improved acres, well stocked, and had refused $16,000.00 for it. We spent a pleasant two hours with our boomer friend and his family. For genuine, unaffected, all-wool and a yard wide hospitality, ye Oklahoman may be equaled, but not surpassed. Noon that day found us at another farmer's house, and he was equally hospitable; we sat down to a fine chicken dinner, and after the repast we were regaled with piano music by one of the farmer's charming daughters. That night we put up some miles west of El Reno at another farmhouse. The next day we crossed the South Canadian River into the Caddo Reservation, a rather hilly country. We never missed a meal and everywhere we went we were cordially welcomes. We continued our journed to the home of some friends near Hobart, where we stayed several days. Had traveled about 350 miles, and when we left there we went north about 200 miles to see another friend. I didn't know exactly whre he lived, but found him after four days' ride, and making only one inquiry. We were now in that little strip of land known as "No Man's Land," but I want to tell you that it is filled with No. 1 people. After a few days' rest we started west for Central New Mexico, some 400 miles away, with but one chance to stop at friends' some 165 miles west. We took our time, riding from forty to fifty miles a day. We were near Hooker, Okla., one Sunday evening about 4 o'clock, when a storm came up and we took refuge with a farmer. His family consisted of a wife and three as fine daughters as one would care to see. Now, I was never an up-to-date Lothario and had never been much of a "lady's man," but, like all natural and vigorous men, enjoy the companionship if the opposite sex. And strange, too, it may seem to some people, I always looked for girls of education and refinement. I admired these girls for their refined though mirthful ways, and they did their best to entertain us. The oldest girl had a beau in attendance, and before supper he and she entertained with some music; the poor chap's fiddling was excruciatingly wicked and I was certainly glad when supper was announced. The foxy oldest daughter must have read what Napoleon said about winning a man's heart by pleasing his stomach, for that supper was one of the finest I ever ate in my life.

Our host was an honest old Texan and, of course, a Democrat, while his wife was a Republican and a lady of superior intelligence. During the meal we were discussing the merits of both parties, and our hostess asked me if I knew anything about socialism; said she thought from what she had heard of Socialists that they were about as bad as anarchists. Stumpy was an 18-karat rampant Socialist, and to check any bad breaks I told her Stumpy was of that faith, and she apalogized most sincerely for her remark and we had a laugh all around; but I could detect a grin of keen satisfaction from the Texan at seeing his wife so neatly taken in. Stumpy hinted that I could play the violin and after supper, accompanied on the piano by the best-looking daughter, I played with considerable flourish and aplomb. After several selections I started in on that old-time melody known by every fiddler, "The Texas Quickstep," which evoked roars of mirth from the old man.

Having told them from the first that we were going to Hooker that night, we were really going to a friend's that lived west of Hooker, and sure we could find him that night. Our old friend assured use we were welcome to stop with him, but we declined with thanks, and at 9 o'clock that night we left. We stopped by the roadside till morning, then fed our horses and had breakfast, before proceeding some twenty miles to reach friends.

The Teuton as a financier: A boy about 15 came to the door. I said: "Can we get breakfast and get feed for our horses?" The boy put his head in the door and spoke in German, answering: "My father say how much you pay?" "Oh," I made answer, "whatever is right. I don't think we'll have any trouble about the price." The boy then replied: "He say $2.50." I said: "No, that is too much; tell him $1.50." Another lapse of time and he again put his head out of the half-open door. "He say two dollar." I then offered him $1.75, telling him that if that did not suffice we would go on. Another three minutes' conversation in German and the boy said: "Get down, it is all right." After feeding our horses we went into the house. The old man was a fine-looking fellow about 60, with clear-cut features and intelligent face, and did not speak English. The good frau (frou) was over 50, but of tremendous bulk; a slovenly girl of about 14, who kept her old-fashioned bonnet on in the house, helped to throw our breakfast together, which was soon ready. Here is the bill of fare: Light bread, black coffee, two eggs each and corn syrup. The chilly night air had given me the appetite of a mother coyote, and taking out the $1.75, I gave it to the cook and, laying another dollar on the table, I said: "Bring up six more eggs apiece." This was indeed a windfall and the whole family got busy. Even the head of the house condescended to poke up the fire.

The next few days brought us into New Mexico, where we stayed with a friend a month and a half. Late in June we came to Colorado and pulled off the Amity affair, which was tame and featureless; the pursuit "amateurish," the worst I ever saw. The nearest the officers got to a hot trail was when they arrested a prominent cattleman who knew me a few years previous in Oklahoma.

After returning to New Mexico, Stumpy decided that he could not come back; said he wanted to quit for good.

Late in July I started back to Eastern Oklahoma from Central New Mexico, a distance of something over 800 miles, alone. I traveled northeast about 250 miles, so as to strike that 168-mile strip originally called "No Man's Land," and which also joins New Mexico, to rest a few days at a friend's who lived there.

One night late I arrived at Perry, a small station on the Rock Island railroad about thirty miles from Tucumcari. I put up at the only hotel in town and unsaddled and tied to a fence in default of livery stable. I arose early next morning (at 6) and made inquiries about horse feed and was told that Mr. Perry, the owner of the townsite, was the only person from whom I could get feed or water. Despite the fact that I had not eaten in twenty hours, I went at once to forage for my horse. On reaching the house I could see through screens that the family were at breakfast. I asked if I could get water and feed for my horse. Someone from inside re-

Indian children do not cry, laugh or have the common sentiment of paleface children, belongs to the "Mother Goose and Little Red Riding Hood" shelf, for this child certainly had all the attributes. The mother gave him that $1.25, but he threw the money to the ground, and, seeing I was ready to mount, got louder. I could not see the justice of my course in taking this little Indian boy's moccasins for my own boy, especially under such sincere protestations, so I sold them back for 75 cents, and it was worth 50 cents to see this little fellow sit right down with such satisfaction and put them on and start on a trot for a clump of timber 300 yards north of the camp; and as I rode east, I saw a small black head peeking over the high grass at the edge of the timber.

At noon of the same day I stopped at Cantonment, which is a misnomer, as the only thing I saw of a mili-appearance was a squint-eyed Indian policeman with a faded uniform and hungry look. However, up at the school building, where a few teachers, an interpreter and a clerk ate—was called mess—about ten of us sat down to table—an auburn-haired woman of about thirty, who seemed to be mistress of the management; two old-maid school teachers, who did their best toward dignified conversation and deportment; two other teachers, two Indians of perhaps 25 or 30, who tried to ape the ways of the white man by small table talk and manners whose pale cast of talk stripped them of all natural dignity and common sense. Men are no more born equal than they are born the same size and complexion, and you can't make them so by writing it in laws and constitutions.

When we finished dinner I gave the Titian-haired lady a ten-dollar bill, out of which to take the price of my dinner, but she could not get the change in town, so she gave back the bill, saying that I could send the amount by postoffice order. She seemed satisfied I would, or maybe she was a game loser. Anyway, I rode five miles out of my way that evening and through the burg of Longsdale and bought a 25-cent postoffice order and mailed it to her.

The next day I got to a friend's house within a few miles of Guthrie, Okla., and stayed all through August, 1908, to dodge the heat and rest my horse and self. Later on I went to Eastern Oklahoma for about

EDITOR'S NOTE: There was an error in the paging of the original edition. Page 39 should follow page 42.

plied: "Yes, sir, you certainly can, and something to eat yourself." Now, this was western hospitality with elaborate trimmings, but I soon saw why, for the speaker was Rod Perry, an intermarried citizen of the Cherokee Nation, and up to a few months before living in Eastern Oklahoma. I stayed with my old friend Perry a couple of days.

Eating Prairie Dog With the Preachers.

This happened twenty-five or thirty miles west of Guymon, in Western Oklahoma.

I stopped at a windmill to water and asked if I could stay for the night; three or four men were filling barrels with water, and one said that he lived a mile to the north and that I might stop up there. A heavy-set man with him carried a shotgun, also a couple of prairiedogs. We walked on together and on his missing an easy shot, I said: "H—— Let me have that dog-gun." On arriving at the house we had dogs, some old, some young. Learning things fast!—that's what I did. I learned that my partner was a minister of the gospel and had been a missionary across the deep salt; but the knockout jolt came when he and another preacher began skinning those dogs, young and old, for supper. No doubt some of those older dogs had stood on their hind legs and barked defiance to the antelope and buffalo before the days of the Santa Fe Trail. Their bushy tails and hides were thrown to two skinny curs, who proceeded to chew with industrious perseverance thereon. The portion passed in to fry for supper. The aroma of a genuine dog stew not only tickles an Indian's risibles, but stimulates his olfactory nerves and saliva to acute possibilities. But the smell of these ancient pups frying was neither fragrant nor edifying. At supper I ate one piece. Soon we were ready for church, which was one mile northwest, and being among the first arrivals, took seats near the front. There were five minister's present besides the missionary's wife, who was something of a haranguer herself. The first half-hour passed quietly enough, but after that things got warm, with a few fervid testimonials and a sure-enough revival was on tap (tab). You know the kind that makes all the boys and girls holler hallelujah during dogdays and kick their heels up at the country-dances as soon as Jack Frost cools off their foolish heads. I saw I was in for it and at first pretended to look the other way (for after each testimonial an all-round handshaking took place), but soon saw that I was losing out; for the older, bolder and more enthusiastic dames were grabbing me anyway; the timid and prettier ones passing me up. I saw this would never do; I must play the game. This shouting continued until 12 o'clock; the energy of these people of the plains was past normal. I ("the stranger within our gates," as the most noisy of the parsons dubbed me) was called upon for a testimonal; an old Union soldier had just spoken and closed by saying that we all had sinned and come short of the glory of God. I said that the sentiments of the brother preceding were my sentiments, that the associations of the evening should ever remain in happy retrospect, and that the ministers were doing a great work in that community. I still stick to that testimonial. I will tell you why: First, I endorse what the old soldier said about everybody falling short of perfection. Secondly, because I was sitting by the prettiest girl present—not a bad retrospect. Thirdly, if the preachers hold true to form on eating prairiedogs, they will do the community a great favor by cleaning out these pesky creatures.

The second day after, I was passing near the little town of Hardesty on the Rock Island railroad, and not being able to get horse feed from farmers, went by town to feed. As I rode up the only street in town, someone quite a ways down waived me. I rode down and shook hands with my missionary friend, who had drove another route, and was there to dedicate a church. I was taken around and introduced to the family he was stopping with; was invited to dinner and my horse feed. They would not accept a cent; I did not like to sponge, so I donated one dollar to the church. I have forgotten my friend's name, but he certainly was a good sort and a thorough good Christian gentleman. A few days after, I pulled up at a farmhouse for dinner about six or seven miles from the northeast corner of the Panhandle, but in Oklahoma. This farmer was from Minnesota and just returning from pasture; said one of his Jerseys had screwworms from a wire scratch; and, no doubt, seeing that I was mounted on a fine horse and saddle, asked me to go out and help. Ordinarily, I could not throw a rope in the Atlantic Ocean, but always being willing to take a chance, and with the firm belief that if chances are even, I have the best of it, I run my bred hourse, Jeff up by the side of that little Jersey, dropped my rope on and turned off with professional ease. My friend was enthusiastic over my cleverness; said I must have been to lots of roping contests. I told him I had, which was true—but as a spectator. I stayed over night, I think it is five miles north of Gage, Oklahoma, with a man named Grummett, or Grimmett. Anyway, he was a fine man, and I always regret lying to a fellow like that. I told him I was off the Cheyenne Indian Reservation about eighty miles east and that I had been over in the Panhandle country after some horses. It don't take the second look at me to see that I am not a Swede, hence, I always find out where a man is from first, then I know just about how far I can string him. If my host was from Eastern Oklahoma, I was from the Kiowa Reservation in Southwest Oklahoma. If he was from Southwest Oklahoma, of course, I naturally was a Shawnee from Northeast Oklahoma. If they were just a year or so from the states I was a native son, going over to the next town to match a horserace or buy a bunch of polo ponies or collect for a number of horses I had sold the year before. I admit that traveling across the country under cover is not highly conducive to veracity.

I stopped one day at noon not far from Woodard, Oklahoma, and the farmer, who was rather too talkative, asked too many questions. So I told him that I was riding a few days in advance of a bunch of horses that I was selling on one year's time without interest. The fellow swallowed the bait, hook and all; was in such high hopes of getting a new team on a year's time that I was sorry that I had told him anything. He did not want to charge me anything for dinner, but I gave the little three-year-old girl a dollar for conscience money.

As I came through the Cheyenne Reservation and by the postoffice and store named Fonda, I stopped at Indian's Camp to buy my son a pair of moccasions. Being out with Wild West shows has strengthened the theory that the Indians were one of the lost tribes of Israel for these Cheyenne, having all the trading instincts of the "Ikies" (Jews). I fiinally got one pair that suited reduced from $3.00 down to $1.25, and had just paid for and tied them on my saddle, when an Indian boy of about six came up and began to yell, jump and point at the moccasins. The general belief is that five weeks and started west again, coming through Tulsa at night about the 5th or 6th of October of the same year. The second evening for supper I pulled up just west of Ripley, at what is known as the Morehead plantation, where a thousand acres of cotton is grown every year, and to see the swarms of negroes necessary to grow and pick this cotton crop, one could easily imagine themselves away down south, instead of a day's ride from "Bleeding Kansas." I had heard of the Morehead home and hospitality. I found Mrs. Morehead preparing supper, and on inquiring if I could feed self and horse, she said I could, and with a strong Irish brogue, asked my name. I replied "McCoy." That name made a "hit," and the good lady called a man to care for my horse and gave me the latest paper. Of course, it was an imposition, but when one is on the jump you could scarcely expect them to be a stickler for hair-splitting truths. The father and son came soon, both fine gentlemen, the younger Morehead being a college man, also of vast practical knowledge. After supper we had a couple of hours' conversation. While I am satisfied he was too shrewd to swallow all I told him, he was too well-bred to evince any surprise when I left at 10 o'clock at night. On offering to pay for hospitality, he would not thing of taking a cent, but gave me a hearty invitation to call again.

A Duck That Did Not Like Single Blessedness.

As I came on west, it happened that I crossed the South Canadian where Stumpy and I crossed that spring. The river runs about north here. On the west bank and about a mile north of the crossing is a fine pool of water about 75 by 50 feet and very deep. We had camped there in the spring, and seeing two ducks, killed one and ate it; and on this trip, as I rode up I saw that duck had a mate, and by a little waiting, got to kill them both. As well as other conveniences of campers, a stout springboard faced southeast, showing that people had this clear pool for ablutions during summer.

Quite a cornfield to the northwest, but no houses in sight from any direction. It is perhaps 600 yards north to the mouth of Lottle Robe. It was here, at the mouth of Little Robe that happened one of those regrettable and cowardly tragedies of the plains. A party of Comanches—not a "war party," as evidenced by the presence of their women and children—were engaged in the unpardonable crime of killing and drying buffalo meat. An armed expedition from Texas, accompanied by a horde of traitor and renegade Indians, surprised and kelled every Indian in camp. According to their own account, they spared neither age nor sex; and as I rode up the valley, I could see in my mind's eye women and children being ridden down and butchered by those cutthroats, both white and red.

The former owner had cut and stacked the coarse, rank grass where, within the memory of living men, was stained with innocent blood. What excuse, what military necessity, required that these Texans march four or five hundred miles to attack a peaceful Indian village? If we believe in the law of compensation, then the white folks of these United States are SURE in for some bad luck; if not, then the meanest and strongest get the biggest loaf, with no fixed or immutable laws, but a haphazard conglomeration that is liable to skid into oblivion.

I passed the evening previous where Custer trained his artillery on the Cheyenne lodges on the north bank of the Washita, about twenty-five or thirty miles southeast. Appreciating the fact that the red man seemed in hard luck in that locality, I lost no time in getting several miles away.

About 200 miles of Clayton, N. M., and at a sort of a stage stand, I stopped for water. A small boy, seven or eight, was standing by the windmill, and a fine-looking Mexican woman and shikepoke-looking cowboy were coming from cowpen to house with milk. I asked my young friend if that was his parents. He replied that that was his mother. Then I asked: "Where did your father go?" He answered: "He killed hisself about a month ago. I don't know where he went." A country lad of eight years answered what prelates and infidels wrangled over for centuries.

I spent the latter part of the summer and fall of 1908 in New Mexico with a friend. Nothing of note happened. I rode a little every day to keep my horse in trim, practiced shooting with the same regularity, and occasionally went and tried my gun on antelope, and if I missed getting an antelope I would knock down a good, healthy-looking two-year beef. One day I was doing a little scouting around the country, some sixty miles from where I stayed, and came up to a sheep camp and made a request for dinner. The fellow in charge was a fine-looking Mexican with very white teeth and long mustaches. He said the boss said not to feed anybody. Now, to not feed anybody was something new to one acquainted with the spirit and customs of the west. In fair English, he told me that he was willing, but that the boss, only a month from England, was an awful grouch and bulldozer. I said: "Why don't you knock his head off?" "Oh," he replied, "I am not afraid, but then I would lose my job. He always comes by here right after noon."

I told him to go ahead and fix me some dinner; that I would wait for Mr. Johnny Bull, and teach him something of the proprieties and habits of ye free-born Americans. I had not long to wait. I saw the Englishman riding toward us with the up-and-down seat that they effect. A stack of millet was fenced near. I led my horse over, threw the gate down and let him into it. Of course, this was done to exasperate my English cousin. Shortly he trotted up, with a loud bawl about my horse being at the stack. I observed a gun on his saddle, so as I stepped to the door, I brought my two automatics where I could use them quick. He said: "Your horse is destroying my stack." I said: "Who the h—— are you?" "I am the boss of the ranch." "What the h—— do I care if you're boss of ten ranches. You can't come over to the low and menial drudgery of pastry-cook. Nonsense, enough; and to my story. I had ample time to read from the prison library, and all papers and magazines I could afford. I made no attempt at special study, but tried to get an intelligent comprehension of what the best minds of all history had thought. I soon realized that it was not worth while for me to try to remember language, style, or dates, but to grasp the ideas in concrete. What caused me to come to this conclusion was, after I had finished reading Patrick Henry's Defi to the English and was trying, with closed book, to repeat some of its thrilling passages, I found I was too thick-headed for that sort of thing and gave up in disgust. I realized and consoled myself with the fact that Mr. Henry had intended to convey the fact that "We'll kick the d—— English into the sea or get ourselves killed," and that was all the facts necessary for me to know.

In 1902, I was pardoned by President Roosevelt; quite naturally I am one of the most ardent admirers of the Lion-Tamer, and as a practical and living evidence, I offer Roosevelt Starr, my only son and heir, now 9 years of age. But I am getting ahead of my story again, and it might be well to say that in September, 1903, I married Miss Ollie F. Griffin, a part Cherokee, and a girl of much refinement and culture. Hence the young Roosevelt Starr, now 9, and weighing over 80 pounds.

After my pardon I went back to Tulsa where I engaged in the real estate business, and resided until 1907; then we moved to a small town, Skiatook, only six miles from my allotment. I took my wife and young Ted to the inauguration of Hon. C. N. Haskell. I am never blase when there is something of interest happening. It was a perfect day—just enough of the military to lend color to the scene. Crack bands from all over the state were there and at their best, and the crowds were in gala attire. We made our way to the Carnegie Library where the inaugural exercises were to be held, myself and family standing near the front where the governor and party would stand. As the governor stepped forward to take the oath of office and deliver his address, I held my small son high above the crowd to see the first governor of Oklahoma. Altho' not of the same politics, I had voted for Haskell because the Republicans had the effrontery to ask decent people to vote for a carpet-bagger, and I had had enough of that tribe. And when Governor Haskell spoke so feelingly of the state's duty to the Indians and gave the Indian Orphan Band the place of honor in the parade at the exercises later in the day, I was glad I had voted for him; racial pride and welfare triumphed over political faith. In addition, Robert L. Owens, himself a Cherokee, took oath of office for U. S. Senator from Oklahoma; and all around the Governor and his party were dark-haired men and women, prima-facie evidence that the Red-man intended to help guide the ship of state. I'll admit I went away feeling rather proud and chesty, for I was living an upright, honest life,— proud of my home and family, and interested in all things pertaining to the welfare of my fellowman.

A few days later I learned from what I believed to be a reliable source, that the state of Arkansas had made requisition to the Governor of Oklahoma for my person for robbing the Bentonville, Ark., bank in June, '93, over 13 years back. Having had some experience with Arkansas juries and courts and feeling that a community that would hound a man for a past offense after years of proper conduct, could scarcely be expected to give him justice, I made up my mind that I would NEVER take the chance of having to go back, and took to the "tall and uncut." I preferred a quiet and unostentatious interment in a respectable cemetery rather than a life on the Arkansas convict farm where the lash and bloodhound are the primary accessories of gentle persuasion. After a time spent in bitter meditation on the scurvy trick FATE had played on me, I proceeded to dig in and break law. I can see now what a foolish thing it was to do, but at the time I was hostile, and bitter against fate. All the past wrongs seem to rise up and cloud my better judgment. My reason seemed to leave me, and I simply went to pieces. Imagine my shame and humiliation, and utter dejection when I learned a couple of months later that Governor Haskell had absolutely refused to give me up, and had I stayed to face the music, I might now have held a place of honor and influence with my own people instead of occupying a prison cell. Influential friends had convinced the Governor that I simply could not get justice if extradited. This period of my life I shall always be bitterly ashamed of; I betrayed the confidence of my friends and the Governor, but I DID NOT know that friends were working for me, nor did I doubt but what the requisition would be ignored, until AFTER I had again broke the law. Of course, I then had to stay a fugitive from justice. My friends used poor judgment in telling me anything at all about the requisition; however, I shall always feel just as grateful as if their effort had brought about years of honorable life, instead of the present condition of things. During the fall and winter of 1907 and the early part of '08, I stayed under cover in Oklahoma. I still had many friends who would shield me. In the spring of '08 the papers credited me with having again got off the reservation with forty kinds of war paint on,—of course we must always allow our newspaper friends considerable latitude. Hell had broke loose, and somebody had to be charged with the crimes; what more natural than that I should be the fall guy, since I was at large, and my whereabouts unknown? The same old story of giving a dog a bad name. Two banks were robbed in Kansas and Missouri, and two in Oklahoma,—all happened in the daytime and within a few days of each other. I de these charges in toto, and in three of these cases the bandits have since been apprehended and convicted. The papers claimed that I was in all of them, and had me in four different places at the same time. Special correspandents were rushed to these scenes and large bodies of armed men were supposed to be close on my trail. I suppose there were a lot of men looking for me, since I was the "only man loose who could rob a bank," but they were a lot of four-flushers of the rankest type who knew that whoever the outlaws were, they had ample time to get away. I was not in any of the three states where the robberies were committed at that time, but a lot of foolish people said if I was, I could not get away on account of my marked appearance and personalities.

I have nothing but respect for a sworn officer of the law, that does his duty, but for the volunteer fakir, I haven't even respectable contempt; and if through mistake they ever got too near me, I made 'em break the underbrush getting out of range.

In April '08 I left Oklahoma on horseback in company with a party I shall call Stumpy. Our start was made from near Muskogee, and we rode about 50 miles that day. The next day we stayed in the mountains in the Creek country. This was about three weeks after the big uproar, and we were both carrying a rifle apiece, and a 45 colts automatic. The second night we made a light ride, and grass being short, I invaded a farmer's corn-bin. The third night put us out of the country where people knew me, and we decided to ride the balance of the trip in daylight. The third morning at sunrise we were about 12 miles north and 10 miles west of Oklahoma City, and close to the little town of Edmond in one of the finest farming countries I ever saw. A pretentious looking dwelling and huge red barns stood off the road to the left, and I remarked to my companion that right there was where we would feed; for no doubt the owner was an old timer with plenty of country hams, eggs, and oats. As we reached the house, out came a typical Oklahoma boomer of about fifty, white comboy here and run this country. I propose to learn you, you idiot, that we are all the same size in this free domain, and that we eat where we find it and make it a bad place to live for anyone that tries to change said customs." He replied: "Man, you must have taken too much rum," and, turning his horse, beat it back toward headquarters. The Mexican was jubilant. Of course, I called him harder than I have mentioned. The Mexican said: "Senor, you can have anything you want; maybe he will not be so smart now." He gave me a hot lunch. I have not been back, but I'll wager he lost his job for his accommodation.

I went from New Mexico to Arizona in January, and on May 11th, 1909, at a little mining town named Bouse, some sixty miles from the line of Old Mexico, I was arrested. My arrest was effected through the treachery of a resident of Tulsa at that time a resident of Tulsa.

Of course, the newspaper got their usual food for big headlines. I was returned to Colorado to stand trial for bank robbery. The Colorado sheriff was just newly elected. As a matter of fact, he was forty miles away. He and one Fenton actually got within forty miles of me. They, through the newspapers, told all about how they drew their guns and leveled them at my heart, and a lot of that stuff. Personally, I think it pretty hard to point a gun at a man's heart forty miles—but that particular sheriff and whiskey detective said they did. I understand that Fenton has got numerous promotions and credit for effecting my capture. Fact is, the traitor, who was a former city treasurer of Tulsa, had some money of mine. I sent for it and he told Fenton that I was at a certain town in Arizona, waiting for this money. Fenton went to Colorado and brought the sheriff down with him, but stayed forty miles away while the Arizona officers arrested me. The sheriff of Colorado, who won his office by less than ten votes, got re-elected because of his ability to trail me all the way to Arizona and arrest me. It's remarkable how such frauds and hypocrites can get by with that brand.

On my return to Colorado I waived preliminary hearing and employed as counsel Hon. Granby Hillyer of Lamar, Colo. I have never regretted my selection, for I regard him not only as a good lawyer, but a conscientious gentleman. Again the Colorado sheriff showed his little cowardly nature. Prowers county had just finished a new jail at great expense to the taxpayers, but for fear of the consequences if I escaped while under his care, Mr. Cold Foot Simpson got an order from the court and had me transferred to Pueblo, and with strict orders to let me see nobody, the res was that I was put in the solitary condemned cell and kept there from June 8th to November 24th and my bond fixed at such an exorbitant figure too, I had no chance to give.

Several friends from Oklahoma came to Pueblo to see me, but were denied admission to the jail. The sheriff at Pueblo said he had strict orders from the sheriff at Lamar not to let me see anyone. It didn't make any difference what I had done, they had no right to put me in solitary confinement and the condemned cell before I had a trial; not apt to increase a man's respect for law and order nor that intangible thing they call society. No fair person will hardly blame me if I feel a little peeved over such treatment.

I was brought to Lamar about the last of November and pleaded guilty. Received a sentence of from seven to twenty-five years at Canon City, a very beautiful, charming summer resort, but not a nice place to go with a penal sentence hanging over your head.

My Meeting With Warden Tynan.

As I entered the prison a squarely-built man with a broad forehead and friendly eyes, said: "Henry, come over here. I want to talk to you a minute." His manner invited confidence; he introduced himself as the warden. We had two or three minutes' conversation. I felt that if a man treated Tynan square, he had nothing to fear, and my relations with him since have more thhan justified my first impression. Thomas J. Tyan has done more practical good toward solving the great problem of penology than all the reformers of all time. Why? Because he starts in while the man is in the penitentiary. He builds up their minds and bodies. He appeals to their sense of fairness and manhood. Every intelligent person knows you can't make a man better by harsh treatment, bad food and foul air. I said Tynan started in while the men were under his care. That's precisely his way. His honor system, at first ridiculed by the newspapers and sneered at by the police, has long ago passed the experimental stage. It's a success, and those who knocked now have to admit the warden knew what he was about. Seven states that I can recall have adopted his honor system. It's easy to say "Me too," but it took a brave soul to say to the world: "I am going to give these poor fellows a chance," and he did and the men under him have amply upheld his contention.

A word about the honor system. A prisoner is allowed to go many miles, yes, often 200 miles, from the penitentiary without armed guards, to work on the roads. All between him and his liberty is his word not to run away. To the ordinary person it would seem a joke to send a man with many years to serve, where he could walk away at will, but it's a fact that the percentage of runaways is so small as to be negligible. I worked on the road for over two years and the last sixteen months acted as night man of the camp with a gun, horse and saddle at my disposal. To the average person who has gleaned opinion of me from newspaper writers, it would mean murder, bank robbery and every crime in the calendar. Truth is, I stayed it out.

A lot of people will be curious to know about certain things, so I'll ask and answer. What is your politics? Haven't any. Your religion? Same. Do you think you have led a correct life? No, but it's as good as some others that are holding office. Don't you think society is going to the dogs? No, I don't; it never was away from them. Don't you feel that it's a great crime to take people's money? Yes, I know it's wrong, but I am only a small theif; the lawyers take it all away from me, and still I go to the penitentiary. The big thieves never go to the pen, and besides, they keep what they steal. For that reason I feel much abused.

THE MAN WHO LOVED BANKS

From Arkansas *Gazette,* Little Rock, Sunday, February 27, 1921.

When they buried Henry Starr in the little cemetery at Dewey, Okla., last Friday, there ended the story of a bandit as picturesque as ever poked a six-gun under the nose of a frightened small-town cashier in all this Western Country.

Starr's deathbed boast to the doctor at Harrison, Arkansas, a day or two before he died from a wound inflicted during an unsuccessful attempt to raid the People's State Bank there, that he had "robbed more banks than any man in the United States," is accepted here beyond a doubt by men who have known him ever since he was a romping cowboy riding a range where Tulsa now stands. And that was nearly thirty years ago.

The fatal ending of the second raid that Starr ever attempted in Arkansas — the first was at Bentonville back in 1893 — has set these old-time friends of Starr to reminiscing. And many are the tales of his prowess, cunning, marksmanship and inevitable good humor and kind-heartedness that are recounted.

According to Starr's own story of how he, a well-educated young Cherokee, who had been educated from the government Indian school at Tahlequah, Okla., chanced to turn outlaw, he was driven to it by unfair peace officers. Working as a cowboy on a ranch between Nowata and Bartlesville in 1892, Starr, then 19, was arrested on a charge of horse stealing and spent several months in jail before a trial at which he was acquitted. Starr said the horse in question strayed about the pasture of the ranch where he was working and was there for several days before turned into the pasture. When nobody claimed the animal after a few weeks Starr mounted it one day and rode to Nowata. The owner of the horse saw him, recognized the animal and had Starr arrested as a thief.

"When they let me out I was bitter against the world," Starr said. "I decided that if they sent people to jail when they had violated no law they couldn't do more to a criminal. Having been branded a criminal, I thought I might as well be one in fact.

"I was only a kid and father and mother had brought me up to think it was an awful disgrace to be in jail. They chained me to a bed that time. That was a bad thing to do to a kid. I was innocent. When I was released I felt that I might as well be dead as disgraced. I came out of that jail with blood in my eye."

From that day until the day he died, Henry Starr was an outlaw. Sometimes he was not "wanted" for anything in particular. But those who knew him best don't believe he ever really reformed. It was simply in his blood to rob banks, just as it was to gamble, they say. Never a winner at cards, Starr's invariable habit when he had made a stake was to hunt a poker game where, regularly, he turned over what money he had to those with whom he gambled. But despite his lifelong association with gamblers and gambling games, he was never known to hold up a game. He just seemed to have an irresistible desire to gamble, especially at poker, and the only way he could get money fast enough to satisfy his craving for cards was to get it in large bunches from "helpless" country banks.

"Henry just figured that the banks owed him what he could take from them, is the way I look at it," remarked one old-time friend of the outlaw. "I don't believe he thought it was wrong. I know he thoroughly enjoyed raiding. He's told me of how he laughed inwardly until he hardly could control himself at the enormous fright some victim banker would show when Starr and his men would step in and take charge of all the loose currency with the 'hands up and hands steady' that Starr always sung out."

Starr was recklessly bold. He took many chances. That probably accounts for the fact that he was wounded in more than one raid and captured several times. He was inclined to underestimate the danger of death or apprehension.

In all his career there probably is no better illustration of Starr's daring and his contempt for the law than a short chapter soon after his release from the Colorado State prison in 1913. He was paroled by the governor of Colorado, conditionally. One of the conditions was that he was not to set foot in Oklahoma, the scene of most of his depredations. Starr lingered in Colorado for a few brief months. Then he slipped away from the state and came back to Tulsa. Taking the alias of "R. L. Williams," the name of a candidate for governor, who later was elected, he rented a little bungalow at 1534 East Second Street. The gas and light meters and the telephone at the Starr home were listed in the name of "Laura Williams" Starr's wife. Starr kept out of sight in the daytime, for just two doors from him on the same street lived Jim Woolley, then Sheriff of Tulsa County. Across the street from him was a church. Next door to him was one of the city's largest ward schools, and every day hundreds of children played in the back yard of the outlaw at recess.

At this time there was a primary election campaign growing hot in Oklahoma. Robert L. Williams, J. B. A. Robertson, Al Jennings, another noted ex-bandit, Charles West and Robert Dunlop were seeking the Democratic nomination. Probably intending to muddle the situation if possible for Williams, who was the favorite, Starr had his "adopted name" of R. L. Williams placed on the ticket. Probably he also hoped to improve the chances of his old friend, Al Jennings. At any rate it did cause somewhat of a mixup, for there were two Williams on the ticket that was voted on at the primary — "Robert L. Williams," who was nominated and just plain "R. L. Williams," who in reality was none other than the outlaw and fugitive, Henry Starr. This also leaked out later after Starr had been wounded and captured in a raid on two banks at Stroud in 1915. It has been generally accepted as true by men who know Starr, but, so far as can be learned, is here printed for the first time.

Men who associated more or less with Starr when he was not "scouting" — some of them of part Cherokee blood and citizens of high standing in Tulsa — believe that Starr from his home on East Second Street directed most of the bank robberies that were so numerous in Oklahoma along about that time. They don't believe he was living here in selcusion for nothing for the many months elapsing from the time he came here until he was shot down and captured at Stroud in 1915. His deathbed statement that he had "robbed more banks than any man in the United States," bears out this theory, they say.

Moreover, they believe he was just as busy at his old trade from the time Governor Robertson paroled him in 1919, until he was shot and mortally wounded at Harrison, Ark., as ever in his life — but that he simply kept his tracks well covered and managed to evade capture. A veteran ex-officer who knew Starr well in the old days went to the chief of Police of Tulsa a few months ago, during a wave of daring and successful bank robberies, and told him there were things about several of the robberies that made him believe it was Henry Starr up to his old tricks. The chief was impressed with the theory, but they could get nothing on Starr.

The eyes of Henry Starr were first opened on December 2, 1873, at Fort Gibson, I.T., near the United States military cemetery. His father, George (Hop) Starr, was a half-breed Cherokee, and his mother, Mary Scott, a quarter blood. He attended the Cherokee Indian mission there until his 11th birthday, when he left school, following the death of his father. The death of his parent threw upon the shoulders of the young Indian boy the duties of caring for his mother and two brothers. Two years later the mother married again, and while Henry strove to get along with his stepfather, he found it impossible, so left home and became a cowboy on one of the large cattle ranches then scattered over the Cherokee Nation.

He became friendly with a gang of youths who were regarded as "wild" many petty offenses being laid at their doors, and often the federal officers would make a raid on the gang. On one occasion Henry was arrested and accused of theft, the deputy marahals attempting to "third degree" him. Starr often made the statement that the shame of false arrest so angered him that eventually he grew to hate any man who sought to carry out the law.

In 1892 the express office at Nowata was robbed. The robbery was done by a party of masked men, who rode away on horseback. One of the robbers rode into a wire fence and was thrown, the horse running away. The animal was found later with a saddle which Henry Starr had borrowed from a friend. A few weeks later Starr returned to Nowata. Floyd Wilson, a deputy Marshal and special officer for the Iron Mountain, attempted to arrest him for the robbery.

The men rode up to each other on horseback, both drawing their revolvers, and at close range they fought a duel to the death. Starr proved to be the better shot and Wilson fell.

With others Starr in January, 1893, shot up the town of Choteau, I.T., robbing two general stores and the depot. Several days later the same gang robbed the general store and depot at Inola, I.T.

Starr's first bank robbery was at Caney, Kansas, on March 25, 1893, when he and Frank Chaney rode into the town and "stuck up" the Caney Valley National Bank for $4,900. The notoriety that he got out of the bank robbery brought scores of lesser known outlaws to his side and by April, 1893, he had formed a real gang.

On May 5, 1893, they held up a Katy passenger train at Pryor Creek, getting $6,000 and a consignment of cut diamonds. Their next exploit was to ride into Arkansas and rob a bank at Bentonville of $11,500 on June 6, 1893. Soon afterward the Starr gang broke up.

About this time Starr discovered that officers were closing in on him, so he started for the West. He met his sweetheart, Miss Mary Morrison, of

Nowata, in the Osage hills, and in a covered wagon they started for Emporia, Kansas, where they expected to take a train for California, get married and never return to the Indian Territory. At Colorado Springs they were overtaken by detectives. With them was "Kid" Wilson, another desperado, wanted in the Territory.

Starr and Wilson were taken to Fort Smith, Arkansas, then the seat of the federal court having jurisdiction over the Indian Territory. Starr was tried for the murder of Wilson, convicted and sentenced to be hanged. Prominent members of the Cherokee Nation worked valiantly and succeeded in getting the young Indian a new trial. After a delay of two years, he was sentenced to 13 years in the federal penitentiary at Columbus, Ohio.

While waiting to be taken to Columbus, a strange incident occurred in the Fort Smith jail.

"Cherokee Bill," a notorious outlaw, a mixture of Indian, Negro, and white blood, occupied a nearby cell awaiting trial for murder and train robbery. One afternoon when a guard came to lock the cells he found the door of the cage occupied by Cherokee Bill blocked by the bad man's foot. A moment later the guard was shot dead. Someone had smuggled a revolver to the bandit.

Jail attendants did not fancy entering the bad man's cell, and while they were determining means of obtaining Cherokee Bill's gun, Starr suddenly volunteered to get it.

Without a word he walked down the runway to Cherokee Bill's cage, swung open the door and entered. The officers, safe around a corner, listened attentively but heard only a faint whispering. A moment later Starr stepped out, locked the cell and delivered the bad man's gun to the officers.

Starr never told how he persuaded the murderer to give up the gun, but it was believed that a sort of Free Masonry that existed between the Cherokees gave Starr control over the mixed-blooded Cherokee Bill. His lips were sealed about what took place between them. A few weeks later Cherokee Bill was hanged.

When Starr had served eight of the 13 years of his sentence, the story of how he disarmed Cherokee Bill came to the attention of President Theodore Roosevelt and he pardoned him.

During his eight years of incarceration at Columbus, Starr devoted himself to reading, particularly in law. He announced on leaving the penitentiary that he intended to settle down on his farm near Tulsa and try to obtain a degree as a lawyer.

While at Columbus he became acquainted with Al Jennings, another Oklahoma outlaw, who has succeeded in "going straight." That Starr actually intended to live straight is what his friends say, but he made a solemn promise to President Roosevelt that he would be a good man in the future.

"I meant it," said Starr. "Why, I named my boy after Roosevelt — Roosevelt Starr."

After being pardoned he married Miss Morrison, who with his mother, had worked indefatigably in getting him freed. Starr opened up a real estate office in this city and did well, but the monotony of it soon palled on him. In 1907 he moved to Skiatook.

Starr and his wife were among the notables at the inaguration of Charles N. Haskell as Oklahoma's first governor in 1907.

While Starr believed that he had successfully beaten back his criminal inclinations, the state of Arkansas had not forgotten the Bentonville bank robbery. It had an indictment hanging over Starr and when Oklahoma became a state the Arkansas authorities asked Governor Haskell to honor it.

While Haskell was pondering on the application, Starr was pretty uneasy. One day he had a friend call up the state capitol. Later this friend telephoned to Starr "He hasn't granted it." But Starr misunderstood. He thought the message was, "he granted it," and he fled West.

It was about this time that Starr is known to have been rejoined by the pal of his younger days, "Kid" Wilson. Together they went to Colorado for the second time and again it eventually proved their undoing. In June of 1908 they robbed a bank in Amity, Colo., and escaped. But after "scouting" for some months in the mountains of Colorado the two bandits quarreled and separated, so Starr later told friends here. Starr said he was afraid Wilson "was going nutty." He grew to fear violence at Wilsons hands.

Kid Wilson disappeared and has never been seen or heard of since so far as anyone in Oklahoma knows. Starr, in telling of this to an old time friend who told it to the writer for the first time after Starr's death at Harrison, significantly said, "Wilson won't bother anyone else."

Leaving Colorado after he and Wilson had split up, Starr went to Arizona. He was safely away from the Colorado officers. But he had an interest in a Tulsa County Indian allotment, and he wrote a real estate man here to dispose of this interest and send him the money, about $450. He trusted this man, whom he had known since childhood. But the trust was misplaced. Starr had furnished the man with his Arizona address and alias. Instead of sending Starr the money, the real estate dealer informed the Colorado authorities where he was and an officer was sent for him, found him and took him back to Colorado. He was sentenced in 1909 to serve 25 years in prison, but after he had served just four years the Colorado governor paroled him. Although his parole provided that he was not to set foot in Oklahoma he quickly decided to risk it here and returned.

His life in Tulsa preceding the Stroud robbery in 1915, which resuled in his wounding and capture, has been mentioned already in this story. On March 27, 1915, Starr and several men robbed two banks at Stroud, Lincoln County, Oklahoma. Of this robbery, Starr afterward said,

"I staged the Stroud robberies for my son. I wanted to make a stake for him. I wanted to make a big haul, fix the boy out and go off somewhere and be forgotten."

The Stroud affair was daringly planned. The robbers rode into town, tied their horses to the stockyards fence, left one of their number in charge and proceeded to the two banks. Over $5,000 in currency was taken from the two.

As the bandits were escaping, Paul Curry, a 15 year old boy, ran into a butcher shop, grabbed up a sawed off rifle and fired at them. The bullet struck Starr in the leg, shattering it. As he fell, Curry shouted to him, "Throw away your gun, or I'll kill you." Starr complied. Louis Estes, another robber, was caught, but the others escaped.

"I am a bank robber, and have been caught; that's all there is to it," said Starr.

His sentence to the Oklahoma prison for 25 years for this raid turned out just as all other prison sentences he had received. He soon won the confidence of the penitentiary officials, and by his straightforwardness and seemingly sincere promises to reform soon had the way paved for another release. It came in 1919. Governor Robertson believed that Starr had had enough of it. He was willing to grant the parole when the petition for it reached the statehouse, bearing the endorsement of the prosecuting attorney, the judge who presided at the trial and most of the jurors who convicted him.

"There's more money in the moving picture business than there is in bank robbing," remarked the Lincoln County prosecutor. "There's certainly no reason why crippled old Henry Starr should hit the trail again."

And Starr went at the motion picture business with great vim. A company was speedily formed to produce a picturization of the famous Stroud robbery, which was one of the most spectacular in the history of Oklahoma. It was re-enacted, even down to the shooting of Starr by Paul Curry, the 15 year old schoolboy, who later won a distinguished service decoration for bravery in action in France. Starr made considerable money out of the picture. He was the leading character in a couple of pictures that followed this one.

"He threw away a wonderful opportunity." This is what George Davis, a moving picture man of Tulsa, said about Starr. Davis had advised Starr somewhat in the days when the ex-bandit was rehearsing the story of his own life at Stroud, called "The Debtor to the Law."

According to Mr. Davis, Starr only recently had received a flattering invitation from a Western movie concern to join them in staging a bank robbery, after which the officer indicated that possibly they would engage him for other Western robberies.

Starr was considering the offer when he went to Harrison, Arkansas, to his death.

Davis stated that he believed that Starr went back to bank robbing soon after being paroled by Governor Robertson in April, 1919. While Starr was taking "pictures" at Stroud he made a trip to Chandler and by a strange coincidence a Chandler bank was robbed, and later he went to Davenport and a Davenport bank also was held up.

"No one ever suspected Henry Starr of these robberies, and I don't know that he was implicated in them, but it certainly sounds strange," said Mr. Davis.

Starr always bore the reputation of excelling at whatever he did. He was a crack shot with a pistol. Once a friend asked him to demonstrate his skill. Starr stepped to the side of a pond, took a pistol in each hand, and for some time practiced shooting off the heads of turtles as they protruded from the water. During his several terms in prison he always studied for the bar. Those who know him well declare their belief that he could have stood the bar examination and could have qualified as a lawyer in Oklahoma when he left Colorado in 1913.

The story is told that Starr was also an expert at the modern art of camouflauge, though he knew it by no such name. Starr himself told this story. He said that when he robbed the bank at Tyro,

Kansas, back in 1893, he was riding a cream-colored buckskin pony. Before riding into the town, Starr carefully gave his horse a coating of black paint, on which he plastered white spots. He said he often made use of such ruses. Many times his only disguise when staging a robbery would be a fake mustache, or shaggy eyebrows, or a beard. He seldom made use of a mask.

A careful study of Starr's career results in the conclusion that he simply couldn't resist the lure of the outlaw life. He knew that it was to his interest to stay straight, but the call pulled him on. Starr gave a good imitation of the fight he was making in an interview with a newspaper at Muskogee on July 4, last.

"All young men should know crime is a losing game, no matter who the players may be," he said. "I would not take $17,000,000 to again face the agony I have endured."

As he spoke Starr drew his chair closer to his interviewer. His voice sank almost to a whisper as he said in a voice more solemn than he had used before, "But once a fellow falls it is hard to rise again."

Three times before he was shot down at Harrison, Arkansas, Starr had walked from the valley of death. Twice he was sentenced to be hanged and his life saved by commutation of his sentences. A few years ago he was wounded by a boy at Stroud, Okla., during an attempt to rob a bank. Starr blamed a woman for his downfall then, after he had striven to "beat back."

In all Starr served 17 years and eight months in prison, according to his own accounting.

* * * * * * * * *

HENRY STARR, CHEROKEE
The Cherokee King of Bank Robbers
by Leonard Saxon

The only time I ever saw Henry Starr and spoke to him was after the Stroud, Oklahoma Bank Robbery when he was a prisoner in the State Penitentiary at McAlester, Oklahoma. I was there to pay a visit to that institution and see the sights, but not as a culprit myself! And so I was being shown about the place by a friendly guard when we met and spoke to Henry Starr who passed us to join a group of others.

When he had passed by us, the guard asked me if I knew who that man was; and of course I had to say no, as I had never seen him before that brief moment. But I knew about his outlaw record as the Cherokee King of Bank Robbers in Oklahoma and elsewhere. Henry was raised at Fort Gibson, Oklahoma — and I in another part of the Cookson Hills at Blackgum — where also lived Redbird Smith, Chieftain of the Cherokees, and a large family of Indian sons named John, Sam, Richard (Dick) and others — just across the hills from us. They were much older than I, but were personal friends of the noted outlaw themselves. He often visited the Smiths and was attached to Richard who was a boy friend of my sister Viola.

Richard told me later that Henry often asked him to join ranks with him in outlawry. But in someway, Richard's better judgment saved him from final disaster; and he lived to attend the funeral of Henry Starr later on. And it was not very long after Henry had paid them a visit, shortly before the Bank Robbery at Harrison, Arkansas, and had asked Sam Smith for a small loan of twenty dollars. Sam could not give the money to Henry, and said he was broke himself; and so Henry said he understood okay.

Henry Starr loved money, but he was always broke. He avoided violence as much as possible, and was not a blood thirsty killer himself. He always claimed that he had to kill Deputy U.S. Marshal Floyd Wilson in self-defense or Wilson would have killed him. For that crime he faced Judge Parker, the 'Hanging Judge' at Fort Smith in 1893, and was there with Cherokee Bill when he killed a guard at the jail. But Henry persuaded Bill to yield up the gun and took it to the officers. That brave deed won for Henry a pardon!

Richard Smith told me that Henry Starr explained his outlawry by saying: "The only difference between me and the bankers is that they rob me with a pencil, and I rob them with a gun!"

Above is a photograph of Lorene Hughes, the young girl who witnessed the robbery of the Stroud, Oklahoma bank by outlaw Henry Starr. Following is her eye-witness account of this event, and hers is probably the only such incident ever recorded by a child who walked into a bank while it was being robbed by a renowned bandit.

"It had been my habit to drop in and see Miss Nellie Neil, cashier at the bank, so on this Saturday morning went in after mother had come to work at my dad's store next door to the bank. When I walked in I hesitated at the door, seeing several strange men there.

" 'Who is that?' one of them asked. It was the leader Henry Starr.

" 'Get out little girl,' the man said after I told them I was from next door.

" 'Better let her stay,' Mr. Patrick said. 'She might say something and cause trouble.' He was an officer of the bank.

" 'O.K. kid. Stick around for the big show.'

"The men continued sweeping money in bags. And Henry no longer pointed a gun at Mr. Patrick, whom he had threatened to shoot if he didn't open the Time Deposit Vault. They said he wouldn't shed blood before a child as he had one of his own, a little boy.

"When they had finished with the money, he told the others it was time to go. 'We're robbing the other bank too, we're meeting the others down there.' He told the bank employees he was going to march them down the alley. He put me on a stool and poured some pennies in my lap, and told me to wait and he would be back and we would get some ice cream. Later my mother came in, hearing the bank had been robbed, found me white as a sheet, sitting there and hanging my head.

"In the meantime word had gotten around that both banks were being robbed, and citizens had gotten whatever guns they could, and there had been a fight with the robbers as they backed toward their horses at the railroad yard.

"A seventeen-year old boy, Paul Curry, had gotten a hog gun at his father's store, slipped up the alley and had wounded Henry Starr. His men had let him lie when he signalled them to go on. He was carried upstairs to a doctor's office over the bank. After his wounds were dressed he was removed to the county jail and sentenced to prison later on.

"He was later paroled when he was supposed to have reformed. He went back to Stroud with a film company to make a picture of the double bank robbery. Another girl of my age at the time, five years old, took my place in the film. Someone pointed me out in the crowd watching, and Henry Starr came over and handed me a dollar, telling me to get that ice cream he had promised me years back and to take some friends along."

CHAPTER 3

The Hanging Judge's Hangman

"Killing a man? Hell, that's nothing at all!" the notorious Manning Clements would snort when asked how he felt about such a chore.

A known hired killer, Clements, a relative of Wes Hardin's usually was paid $300 or thereabout for silently disposing of some unwanted person, a fee that seemed perfectly reasonable to him. It is likely he was paid a bit more for disposing of Pat Garrett, although many claim that someone else killed the old-time lawman.

But there was another man who charged much less than Clements. He did his gruesome work in a legal way, and in the course of his business sent more than eighty men on their swift journeys into the unknown, dangling from the end of a rope. At times, he hanged as many as six at one drop.

The man who cut Manning Clements' price spent twenty years in his business, and on retiring went around the country giving lectures and exhibiting the tools of his bizarre profession. He would also demonstrate, with some particular part

of his equipment, just how and in what manner it had been used in the successful accomplishment of a specific job.

"It's only a matter of knowing how," he would say in his talks,"and a fellow that don't know how, shore ain't got no business in the game. He only botches up things."

I've sometimes imagined myself as listening to a conversation between Mr. Clements and his rival, the man who had had the temerity to cut the standard rate of $300 per killing to $100.

"I know, George, but hain't right for you all to go and cut rates on me like that. 'Sides, you hain't a-takin' half the chances I am."

"Wal, maybe you all are right, Manning, p'haps I shouldn't cut rates on you all, and I'll hafta agree with you all 'bout taking chances, the way you do a job is a heap more dangerous, and you aire a-stickin' yore neck out every time you do a job. But it all works out 'bout even in the long run. You see, I've got steady work at $100 per head, and you all gotta step around. I kin see yore point why you charge $300 for a-don' the same job that I only get $100 fer."

The man who got $100 for each job was George Maledon. Maledon was the official hangman for one of the most remarkable men who ever presided in a court of law — the one and only Judge Isaac C. Parker, the famed "Hanging Judge" of Fort Smith, Arkansas. For more than twenty-one years, Judge Parker had judicial power never before or since granted to a judge in the United States.

During Judge Parker's tenure of office, he did see that his "official hangman" had plenty of steady work. In that time, he pronounced the death sentence on a total of 172 persons, of which number 88 were hanged.

Of these 88, Mr. Maledon actually officiated as the hangman in no less than 87. In addition he ran up five more "credits" by killing five men who were foolish enough to imagine they might possibly beat the noose by escaping, for, in addition to being an A-1 hangman, Mr. Maledon was also better than the average with a sixgun.

On only one occasion did Maledon ask to be excused from doing his job as hangman. That was in the case of Sheppard Busby, who, like Maledon, was a former Union soldier. Busby had been a member of the 56th Illinois Regiment, while Maledon had served during the Civil War as a member of the 1st Arkansas Federal Battery. Both he and Busby were members of the G.A.R., and when Busby was sentenced to be hanged, Mr. Maledon went to Judge Parker and asked that a substitute be appointed in his place to hang Busby.

"Excused, why?" demanded Judge Parker.

"He's an ex-Union soldier," replied Maledon.

"Oh, all right, you are excused," said Parker, who also was an ex-Union soldier.

This is the only instance concerning the 88 men who were hanged during Parker's time on the bench, where Maledon did not personally assist in sending the doomed man on his way.

George Maledon was a strange, silent, peculiar man. It is said he was born in Germany, near the French border, in 1830, and when still a babe, was brought to this country, where his people settled in Detroit.

In later years Maledon came to Arkansas, where he worked at different occupations and was finally appointed a member of the Fort Smith Police Department. At the outbreak of the Civil War, he joined up with the Union forces and served throughout the conflict.

When the war was over he returned to Fort Smith and was soon appointed a deputy sheriff. Shortly thereafter, when the United States District Court was moved from Van Buren, Arkansas, to Fort Smith, he got a job as Deputy United States Marshal. Maledon liked prison work and when a new hangman was needed, he applied for the position, and for almost twenty-one years was Judge Parker's official executioner.

Maledon was very proud of the efficient and business-like manner in which all his hangings were conducted, and years later, when he had retired and was traveling about with his own tent show showing off his dearly beloved ropes, he would lecture and demonstrate just how the rope should be adjusted around a condemned man's neck.

"You see, the knot has gotta be close up under the left ear to get a quick and sure break of the neck," and he would demonstrate how a body would be propelled through the trapdoor, and how the victim would come to a sudden stop at the end of the rope.

"Why, you-all, with this one rope I hung thirty men; yep, and had another used to hang another eleven. Yep, good hemp. Come all the way from Kentucky by boat, non good 'nuf 'round these parts. I'd take it home, oil it, and stretch it with sandbags and the like until it was about an inch thick."

Maledon seemed to take a sadistic pleasure in handling those ropes as he ran them through his hands and cuddled them.

"Funny thing about ropes," he'd say. "A man who really knows this job of hanging men knows just exactly what kind of rope is best. This hemp is hand woven. I've used it a-plenty and it's always given a satisfactory job," and he would smirk at his bizarre joke.

"It was originally an inch and an eighth, but that's too large so I gave it a good stretchin' before I used it for a job. Now, as you can see it's just 'bout a good one inch 'round. It's about right that way, and I'd not take $50 for the hemp."

He was asked about the hangman's knot.

"I noticed it appears to be extra large, why is that?" asked one spectator.

"I'm glad you-all asked that question," Maledon smiled as he slipped the noose over his own head and pulled the knot up under his own left ear.

"See? I'll show you why the big knot. I place the knot right here, then allow a little slack by draping the rope slightly over the head. See? Like this. Now when the body drops, that slight slack 'nd the knot right up under the left ear, the head is jerked slightly to the side, 'nd the neck is snapped instantly, just like that," and he would snap his fingers dramatically; then wait a minute before going on.

"The right way 'nd the only humane way to hang a man is to break his neck instantly, 'nd of course as painlessly as possible — thus the slight slack laid on the head 'nd the big knot."

He would pause and look around at the amazed audience and then continue.

"I hope that answers your question, 'nd I might go on to say, that in all my experience, with one or two exceptions, the men I have hanged have dropped through the trap, 'nd at the end of the rope, have come up with a sudden snap, the neck breaking." He would rub his hands together and then go on in a matter of fact tone.

"There the body would hang. There would be a little 'nd, in most cases, no twitching of the body. The body would probably turn about a half-turn as the rope twisted a bit, but soon everything would straighten out. The body would become still 'nd in about two minutes or so the man would be dead."

He explained a bit further. "When the man's neck is broken he is unconscious 'nd death is instant or as near instant as death can be. I have broken the neck of every man I hanged. Every one of my hangings has been a scientific job. I have dropped as many as six through at one time, 'nd twice have hanged five at one time, 'nd there wasn't a quiver in the entire sixteen, not even a foot moved.

"There they hung, all in a row, just swaying a bit, all feet about the same height from the ground."

He was asked if he was ever bothered by the "Ghosts" of any of the men he had hanged. He smiled.

"No," he replied, "of course not. I don't believe in ghosts. If there are such things as ghosts maybe I hung 'em at the same time, 'nd besides, I never hung a man that didn't deserve hanging. Most of 'em deserved worse. No, ghosts don't bother me a-tall."

Probably Maledon's worst disappointment came when the murderer of his daughter was sentenced to life imprisonment instead of to death on Maledon's gallows. Maledon's daughter, Anne, had been murdered, but after two trials of her killer, appeals finally cheated Maledon out of the satisfaction of hanging his daughter's murderer. Anne was only 18 when she was shot by a married adventurer named Frank Carver.

Anne Maledon's story is one of the tragedies of our great west. Although one of the prettiest girls in Fort Smith, Anne, as the daughter of the southwest's most famous hangman and a former hated and feared lawman, wasn't exactly popular with some of those who thought of themselves as the "better class."

So poor Anne Maledon became less particular in those with whom she became acquainted. It was thus she got to know Frank Carver. Carver was a smooth talker and was considered unusually handsome by some. It is no wonder then that Anne, already with two strikes on her by virtue of her father's job fell hard for the handsome Frank Carver. Carver was 24 when he met Anne Maledon and she was just past 18.

It was somewhat of a shock to her when she discovered the man she was beginning to love had been brought to Fort Smith on a whiskey charge — selling liquor unlawfully to the Indians. As time passed, Anne began to figure out things for herself. Her neat little room at the Maledon home became a place of planning, and she thought up means to keep a careful check on Carver. When she discovered that the man was a professional gambler as well as a heavy drinker, her only thought was to seek the comfort of her now lonely room, and this she did.

Carver was acquitted on the whiskey charge, and remained in Fort Smith. Although Anne knew the man was a bad influence on her and that she should listen to the pleas of her loved ones, she continued to see Carver. In fact, her love for him seemed to grow stronger instead of dimming. It was as though Carver had cast a hypnotic spell over the poor girl.

The real heart-breaker came the day Anne discovered that the man she loved was already married and the father of two small children. Before this, however, Carver had proposed that she accompany him to Colorado, where they lived for nearly two years as man and wife.

After their return to Fort Smith, Carver still took trips around the country, possibly for gambling purposes or to raise money some way. It was during his absence on one of these jaunts that lonely Anne met Frank Walker, a fine chap who had none of Carver's weaknesses.

As could be expected, Carver learned of this and became insanely jealous. Anne realized that a clean break from Carver was the best thing for her. She refused to agree to Carver's threats and continued to see Walker, with Carver becoming increasingly jealous.

With Anne's refusal to abide by his demands, Carver began to hit the bottle more heavily, at the same time nourishing his jealousy. On the night of March 25, 1895, he met Anne on the street and grabbed her arm.

"Anne, darling, I am going to kill you!"

The startled girl jerked herself free from his grasp.

"What is the matter with you, Frank? Why would you want to kill me when you claim you love me?"

Their conversation was brief, with Carver accusing Anne of being unfaithful to him. She denied the accusation but to no avail.

"I am sorry to do this, Anne," he said, and shot the girl four times and darted away.

In a few minutes he returned, and taking the girl in his arms, he said: "Darling Anne, who did this?"

"You know who shot me, Frank. Why pretend?"

With that Carver let the girl slide from his arms and fled again. Anne was taken to the hospital, where it was found her chances of recovery were slim. From all accounts she accepted her fate like a brave soldier.

The city of Fort Smith was ablaze with fury over the attempt at murder. The general belief was that father Maledon would soon be placing a noose around Carver's neck.

Anne suffered intensely for nearly three months before she passed away. In spite of her weeks of untold misery and suffering there appeared to be a smile of peace and contentment on her pale features when she died.

Carver, naturally, was charged with murder and his trial came up before Judge Parker. Carver was found guilty in short order and was sentenced to be hanged. However, he had retained one of the southwest's most famous criminal lawyers, J. Warren Reed, to defend him, and the attorney found witnesses who were willing to swear that Carver could not possibly have committed the murder.

Reed took a writ of error to the Supreme Court. Judge Parker's decision was reversed and Carver was remanded for a second trial. In this second trial the jury brought in a verdict of guilty with a penalty of life imprisonment.

Anne's father had lived through both trials with only one thought in mind which he showed as he ran his famous ropes through his fingers. He thought that he, as Anne's father, and the most famous hangman of all time, would have the pleasure of springing the trapdoor that would send his daughter's murderer to his doom.

George Maledon never recovered from the terrible disappointment and soon gave up his job as Parker's official executioner. He sold the property in Fort Smith; moved to Tennessee, and on May 6, 1911, passed away.

We were told Maledon received $100 for every man he hanged, so at $100 per head, his payment for the 87 men he sent to their deaths would total $8,700; less, of course, "funeral expenses" of those bodies unclaimed by relatives.

Maledon was one of the most remarkable men of his time, and his job an unusual one that wouldn't appeal to all men.

* * * * * * * *

George Maledon, Official hangman for Judge Parker. Was called "Hangman from Hell." His greatest disappointment in life was the fact that he did not get to hang the man who murdered his daughter.

Members of notorious but short-lived Rufus Buck gang of outlaws. Left to right — Maoma July, Sam Sampson, Rufus Buck, Luckey Davis, Lewis Davis.

Photograph page 106 shows poem written by Rufus Buck on the back of a faded photograph of his mother.

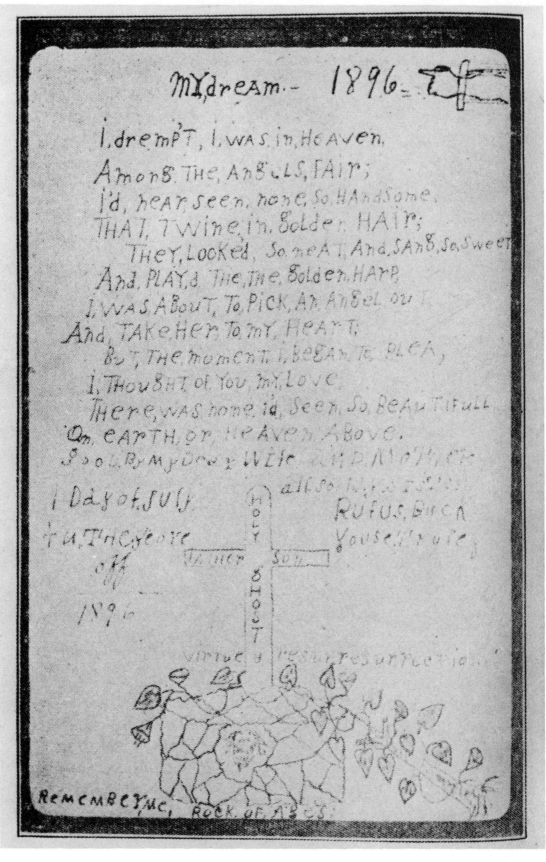

CHAPTER 4

Hanging Judge Parker

Isaac C. Parker was born October 15, 1838, the son of Jane and Joseph Parker, near Barnesville, Ohio, in an area known as Vinegar Valley.

Parker attended the Breeze Hill school as well as the Barnesville Classical Institute. The first mention of Parker as an attorney was made in St. Joseph, Missouri in February, 1861, when he opened a law office. Apparently he was successful as an attorney in the Pony Express town for he was elected city attorney of St. Joseph and re-elected in 1863. It was also in St. Joe that he married a young convent girl named Mary O'Toole. In November of 1868 Parker was elected to a six-year term as circuit judge of the Ninth Judicial District. In 1870 he resigned his judgeship to run for Congress and won. In 1874 he ran for the United States Senate from Missouri and was defeated. The defeat was a serious blow to Parker, and he later approached President Grant and asked for an appointment. Eventually he was appointed judge of the United States District Court for Western Arkansas, located at Fort Smith. Grant told Parker the court had been a disgrace under Judge Story and since Parker had studied the history of the Indians very well, Grant believed he would be just the man to straighten out the problems of the court.

Judge Parker opened his court on May 10, 1875; it was to produce a terrifying and ghastly record of hangings. The first man to dangle from Maledon's ropes was a twenty-one year old Texan named Daniel H. Evans. He was accused of mur-

dering a young man named Seabolt.

With Evans died five other men . . . all hanged at the same time. John Wittington was hanged for the murder of John T. Turner. Samuel W. Fooy was hanged for the murder of John Emmett Neff, a schoolteacher.

A Cherokee named Smoker Mankiller was hanged for the murder of his neighbor William Short.

A Negro farmer named Edmund Campbell was hanged for the murder of Lawson Ross.

James H. Moore, the leader of a gang of horse-thieves, was hanged for his many crimes; he actually boasted of having killed eight men.

At 10:00 A.M. on September 3, 1875, these six men were sent into eternity as Maledon pulled the controlling lever on the scaffold. The hangings never ceased until eighty-eight men had died on the gallows. Probably the most vicious of all who died under sentence from "Hanging Judge" Parker was "Cherokee Bill" Goldsby. The last man to die on Parker's gallows was James Casharago, who was hanged for the murder of Z. W. Thatch. The hanging occurred July 30, 1896.

Judge Parker died early on the morning of November 17, 1896 . . . two months and seventeen days after his court had been abolished. His funeral was the largest that Fort Smith had ever seen. Parker was buried in the National Cemetery in grave No. 4000 . . . the headstone carried no wording other than his name.

J. Warren Reed, frontier lawyer who defied Judge Parker in court room.

"The Hanging Judge", I. C. Parker, 1875.

(Below) U.S. Jail, Gallows and Court House, Fort Smith, Arkansas — "Most Historical Court in the World".

From this bench Judge Parker's famous words rolled across the court room . . . "I sentence you to be hanged by the neck until you are dead . . . dead . . . dead!"

Maledon and his Ropes

Judge Parker's implacable foe, J. Warren Reed, was born December 9, 1849, in Parkersburg, West Virginia, the oldest of nine children. When he was still a young baby the family moved to Williamstown, Wood County, West Virginia. Always alert and eager to learn, Reed became the brightest and most ruthless young man in the county. Later he married a schoolteacher who had studied law, but was unable to become a member of the bar at that time due to her sex. However, she did brilliant work on some of her husband's cases from a background position.

On October 6, 1879, J. Warren Reed was admitted to the bar. He became known as the "lawyer who always won." He was permitted to practice before any court in the land; finally moving to California, where he began to specialize in criminal law.

With Fort Smith brimming with criminal law activity, it was not long before Reed and his wife moved there. He won his first case in defending an Indian named Charlie Keys, who had been accused of killing Larken Powell. This case was tried at Nowata, Oklahoma, and the courtroom echoed with Reed's eloquent defense which lasted twelve hours, and today is considered a classic speech. He won his case.

If he lost a case in the courtroom Reed would take it to the President of the United States. Reed found a working tool when on February 6, 1889, Congress passed an act granting the right of appeal to the Supreme Court of the United States in all cases of conviction where the punishment was death. When a Mexican named William Alexander was convicted in Parker's court for the murder of David Steadman, Reed appealed the case to the Supreme Court which reversed the judge's hanging sentence. Alexander eventually was released from custody; Parker was visibly shaken by having his court overturned.

Reed carried on his legal manipulations; freeing men who probably were guilty, thus galling Judge Parker all the more. He became the richest and most famous lawyer in Fort Smith. However, times were changing. With the abolishment of Parker's court the legal needs of the town subsided. Things became so quiet that Reed moved his offices to Oklahoma. Yet, even this move did not bring him added business. Younger men were taking over; the excitement of the old days was dwindling.

Reed, the man once in high demand, now was having trouble making a living. His next move was to concentrate on writing a book concerning Parker's court. Reed engaged a man named Samuel W. Harman to assist him in writing the book called *Hell on the Border*. The book was not a great success so Harman teamed up with George Maledon, the judge's hangman, and together they toured the country, giving speeches and displaying Maledon's famous hanging ropes. When Maledon and Harman returned to Fort Smith and expressed a desire to take down the gallows to display around the country, the city fathers became so agitated they burned it.

The once famous Reed took to selling his book from door to door, but it was a disgracing business for this proud man. He returned to Muskogee, Oklahoma, where he died on September 8, 1912, and was brought back to Fort Smith, to be buried in Oak Cemetery, less than two miles from the grave of his arch-enemy Judge Issac Parker.

THE THIRTEEN DAY RAMPAGE

The Rufus Buck gang was about the most vicious bunch of outlaws who ever soiled the frontier. Buck was a Euchee full-blood living in the Creek Nation. With him rode three other Creeks: Lewis Davis, Sam Sampson, and Maoma July. Along with them rode another mean character named Luckey Davis, a mixture of Creek and Negro. These men committed more heinous and terrifying acts than any other gang which infested the Indian Territory.

The Buck gang sprang up suddenly near Okmulgee, Creek Nation, flourished for thirteen days, and were arrested. During this flash-in-the-pan existence they made the records of the Daltons and the Doolin bunch sink into insignificance, considering the length of time they operated.

On Sunday, July 28, 1895, this unholy alliance shot and killed a Negro deputy marshal at Okmulgee. With the marshal out of the way the Buck gang murdered and pillaged at will. After this the band raided through the country, terrorizing the citizens wherever they went. Four of the band met a Mrs. Wilson and two young men who were moving her household goods from one point to another. They forced the two boys to ride on and then they brutally assaulted her.

Several days later the five members of the gang went to the home of Henry Hassan, who lived between Duck and Snake Creeks. After forcing the woman to prepare dinner for them, all five of them ravished the wife of Mr. Hassan, holding him at bay with their rifles.

On Berryville Creek the Buck gang met a man

Emanuel (Manning) Clements, the man who killed for money, was expert gunman; killed March 29, 1887 by City Marshal Joe Townsend in the Senate Saloon at Ballinger, Texas. Was Related to John Wesley Hardin. Credit Univ. Okla. Library.

(Right) Rare photo of Roy Dougherty, alias "Arkansas Tom" Jones, Oklahoma bandit with long record of sentences for manslaughter and bank robberies. He was killed by Joplin, Missouri, police in 1924. (Below) Garrison Avenue in Fort Smith, Arkansas, in 1880.

named Shafety and robbed him of his horses and valuables. Later they met a man named Callahan and a colored boy who was riding with him. They robbed Callahan and shot and killed the Negro boy.

The outlaws next visited the home of Gus Chambers, where they fired a number of shots into his home and then stole a horse from the corral. In the locality of McDermott they robbed the Norberg store and the Orcutt store. On Saturday, August 10th, Captain Edmund Harry of the Creek Light Horse (Indian Police), with Tom Grayson, George Brown, and a man named Skansey, accompanied by Deputy United States Marshals Sam Haynes and N. B. Irwin and nearly a hundred citizens of the Creek Nation, ran the outlaws to earth just outside of McDermott. After a fast and furious battle, the Buck gang was captured, with the exception of Lewis Davis, but, he too, was captured a short time later.

The infamous Buck gang was taken to Fort Smith the next day and lodged in Parker's prison. Even the prisoners therein sent up a great clamor, pounding on the walls rattling tin cups against the bars, shouting they did not want the fiendish five admitted to their jail.

During the following week evidence gathered against the Buck gang was placed before the grand jury. The court record shows it thusly:

United States of America, Western District of Arkansas. In the Circuit Court, May term, A.D. 1895.

United States vs. Rufus Buck and Lewis Davis and Luckey Davis and Sam Sampson and Maoma July — Rape. The grand jurors of the United States of America, duly selected, empaneled, sworn and charged to inquire into and for the body of the Western District of Arkansas aforesaid, upon their oath present:

That Rufus Buck and Lewis Davis and Luckey Davis and Sam Sampson and Maoma July, on the 6th day of August, A.D., 1895, at the Creek Nation, in the Indian country, within the Western District of Arkansas aforesaid, in and upon Rosetta Hassan, a white woman, and not an Indian, feloniously, forcibly and violently an assault did make, and her the said Rosetta Hassan, then and there and against her will, forcibly, violently and feloniously, did ravish and carnally know, contrary to the form of the statute in such case made and provided, and the peace and dignity of the United States of America.

E. J. Black, Foreman of Grand Jury
Jas. F. Read, U.S. District Attorney, Western Dist. of Ark.

The prisoners were arraigned on August 20th and the trial set for 8:30 A.M. September 23rd. After all the evidence had been presented, William M. Cravens, one of the five attorneys appointed to defend the Buck gang, uttered what probably was the shortest defense plea ever recorded. He said:

"May it please the court and you gentlemen of the jury, you have heard the evidence. I have nothing to say."

The jury left the courtroom and returned almost at once with a verdict of guilty. Two days later Judge Parker pronounced the death sentence upon the members of the Buck gang. On July 1, 1896, that sentence was carried out after an appeal to the Supreme Court had upheld the decision of the lower court.

Sketched on the back of a faded photograph of his mother Rufus Buck had written a poem entitled "My Dream." Some people have regarded this statement as legend, but we are presenting with this text an exact reproduction of the poem in Buck's own hand.

THIRTEEN MEN THIRTEEN MINUTES

Crawford Goldsby, or rather "Cherokee Bill", was one of America's most vicious murderers; and it is doubtful if more than his personal friends knew Cherokee Bill's real name.

Goldsby was born at Fort Concho, Texas on February 8, 1876. It is somewhat doubtful if a more thoroughbred mongrel was ever born into this world. He was a mixture of white, Mexican, Indian and Negro. His father was a soldier of the famous Tenth Cavalry, colored, of the United States Army. He was of Mexican extraction, mixed with white and Indian blood. Cherokee Bill's mother was Ellen Beck, half Negro, one fourth Cherokee Indian, and one fourth white; thus, Bill was known as a "breed."

Bill's parents separated soon after his birth, and until he was about seven years old, young Crawford lived with a Negro nurse at Cherokee, Kansas for three years. Later still, he was a student at the Catholic Indian School at Carlisle, Pennsylvania until he was twelve. At the age of eighteen he was a big, lusty, burly fellow who had never known what discipline meant.

Soon, as was to be expected, young Goldsby got into trouble. He shot and wounded Jack Lewis, a Negro, and left him for dead, fleeing from the Cherokee Nations with Jim and Bill Cook, two other pretty tough customers. The two Cooks, incidentally, afterwards attained much publicity in the annals of outlawry.

This was early in the spring of 1894. In July of that year Cherokee Bill and his two companions, Jim and Bill Cook, got a woman by the name of Effie Crittenden to draw them their share of the government money being paid to the Indians for the Cherokee Strip. With all this "easy money" in their possession, the three went on a real "bender." They were paid on July 16th, and on the night of the 18th, a posse, composed of the sheriff, who had a Cherokee warrant for the arrest of Jim Cook on a larceny charge, surrounded a house in which the three were holed up. Sequoyah Houston, Dick Crittenden, estranged husband of Effie, Zeke Crittenden, Dick's brother, Bill Nickel, Isaac Greece, and two other men named Hicks and Brackett, surrounded the house.

A gunfight followed. Houston was killed, and Jim Cook was wounded seven times. After Houston fell, the posse withdrew, all except the two Crittenden brothers, who were afraid to turn their backs to depart. They remained and held their antagonists at bay inside the house until darkness, when they too retreated.

It was following this episode that Crawford Goldsby became known as Cherokee Bill. It is said that Lou Cook, asked if he had seen Goldsby, remarked, "No, it was Cherokee Bill." Thus, the outlaw with the name that sounded like that of a movie hero, was henceforth called Cherokee Bill.

Soon after this fight the famous Cook gang of outlaws was organized. It was composed of Bill Cook, Cherokee Bill, Henry Munson, Curtis Dason, "Chicken" Gordon, and later Sam McWilliams, who was known as the "Verdigras Kid." Jim French and others also belonged to the gang at one time or another.

About this very time there occurred the robbery known as the Schufelt holdup. It is said that Cherokee Bill, Jim French, and the Verdigras Kid pulled this job. In this affray a man by the name of Melton was shot and killed, allegedly by Cherokee Bill, who became annoyed when he saw Melton watching him from across the street through a window. The Schufelt robbery took place at Lenapah, Indian Territory in 1894.

Bill was captured by two deputies, Isaac Rogers and Clint Scales after much maneuvering and an attempt to drug him with morphine-filled whiskey. Finally, however, Bill was struck over the head with the barrel of a pistol, the old time maneuver known as "buffaloing" and made famous by Wyatt Earp, and disarmed. One account states that he was betrayed by a friend for the reward, but there is no substantiation to this report.

A huge crowd attended the trial, which opened in February of 1895 before the famous "Hanging Judge" Isaac Parker at Fort Smith, Arkansas. Bill was found guilty and sentenced to be hanged, but appealed his sentence to the Supreme Court through J. Warren Reed, in the meantime being confined to the filthy jail at Fort Smith. A gun was smuggled in to Bill while he was in jail. Bill later said that Ben Howell, believed to have been a confederate of the Doolin and Dalton gangs, smuggled two guns to him on the end of a long pole thrust through the cell window in the dead of night. On July 26, 1895 Cherokee Bill killed Lawrence Keating, a guard, and attempted to escape. He got out of his cell and dashed around the jail exchanging shots with the guards. At every shot he would gobble like a turkey. Finally he was forced back into his cell where he fired at random without exposing himself. Later, at the earnest solicitation of Henry Starr, also a prisoner, Bill gave up his guns and surrendered.

He was then tried for the murder of the guard, Keating, and was of course found guilty and again sentenced to hang.

A rather peculiar feature in the life of this man is the way the number "thirteen" appeared in his career. The figure appears several times at his trial. It took Judge Parker just thirteen minutes to instruct the jury. The jury retired and returned a verdict of guilty in thirteen minutes. Bill, so it is said, had killed thirteen men. A reward of $1300 was offered for his capture. He was first sentenced on April 13th. He killed Keating on July 26th ... twice thirteen. He is said to have fired thirteen shots during his attempted escape and his fight with the guards. The hours occupied in the trial were thirteen. The jurymen and the deputy bailiff who stayed with them numbered thirteen, and there were thirteen witnesses for the prosecution. Bill was finally hanged on March 17, 1896, at 2:13 o'clock in the afternoon. There were thirteen steps to the gallows; thirteen knots in the noose. Are you superstititious? When on the gallows he was asked if he wished to make a last comment. Bill replied, "I came here to die, not to make a speech." Cherokee Bill's only one commendable trait was his undying love for his mother. She went all through the trial with him, never leaving him out of her sight. After Bill was pronounced dead they found over his heart a photo of his mother.

Hanging Judge Isaac Parker in older years.

(Right) First six men hanged by Maledon. (Below) Gavel used by Hanging Judge Parker at his Fort Smith court, presented to him by President U. S. Grant.

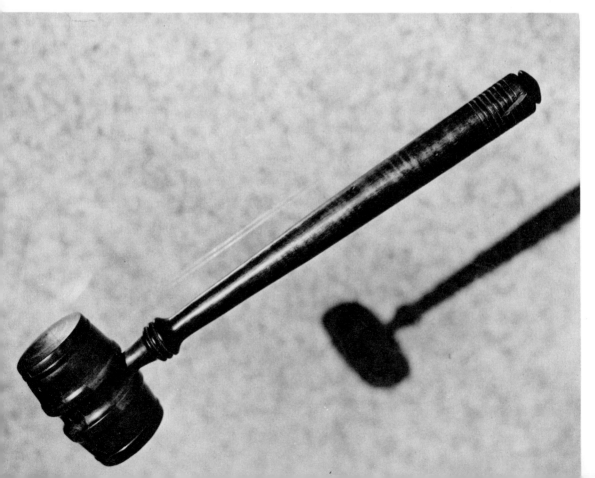

"Cherokee Bill" Goldsby, one of the Old West's most vicious murderers.

(Below Cherokee Bill's single action .45 Colt now at Saunders Museum, Berryville, Arkansas. (Above) Outlaw leader Bill Cook.

(Right) Cherokee Bill's last photograph. Below, his fellow outlaws, left to right — Zeke Crittenden, Dick Crittenden, Cherokee Bill, Clint Scales, Ike Rogers, Bill Smith.

(Left) Al Jennings, train robber. After prison he became prominent lawyer, writer, evangelist. (Below execution of Cherokee Bill.

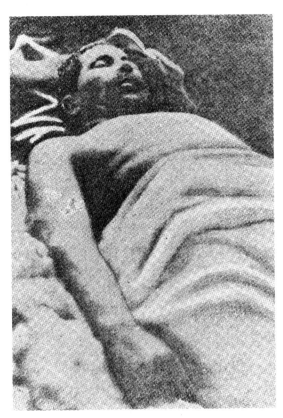

Bandit Ike Rogers in death. Below, U. S. Arms Co. revolver used by "Skeeter" Baldwin.

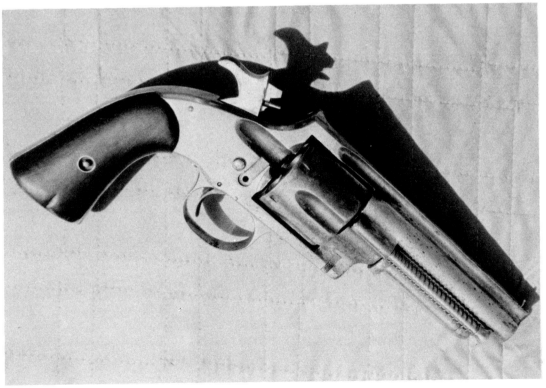

Thurman "Skeeter" Baldwin was member of famous Bill Cook gang. Captured by Texas Rangers, tried in U.S. Court at Fort Smith, he was sentenced to 30-year prison term.

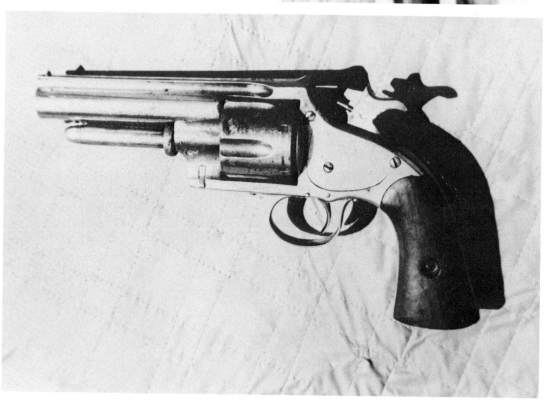

Rare photo of the bold bandit Black Bart, the robber who held up stages with an unloaded gun. Credit photo Wells-Fargo Bank History Room, San Francisco.

CHAPTER 5

Black Bart,

Phantom Stagecoach Robber

When we say that "truth is stranger than fiction," we certainly can apply the term to the legend of Charles E. Boles. Under the alias of Charles E. Bolton, Boles lived in San Francisco, California, as a rich mining man, while obtaining his wealth as a highwayman known as "Black Bart." From all other accounts, Charles E. Boles, alias Charles E. Boulton, alias Charles E. Bolton and Black Bart, was the most elusive and mysterious stagecoach robber ever run to earth by the Wells-Fargo detectives.

Charles E. Boles was a native of Calveras County, New York State, where he was born in 1835. At the age of twenty he joined the ranks of those who had taken the "gold fever" and had headed for California. Three years of hard work in the mines at various spots in the west, and not gaining his fortune, convinced Boles to return east. He settled in Illinois, where he met a young girl of his choice and they were married.

When the Civil War broke out Boles volunteered and was commissioned a First Lieutenant in the Illinois Volunteer Infantry, Co. B, and served throughout the entire conflict. Discharged in 1865, he returned to his family and remained in Illinois for about a year. Boles then set out for Oregon with his wife and three daughters. There he found life not to his liking and set out for Montana. For several years Boles kept in touch with his wife; then all communications ceased.

☞ Agents of W., F. & Co. will not post this circular, but place them in the hands of your local and county officers, and reliable citizens in your region. Officers and citizens receiving them are respectfully requested to preserve them for future reference.

Agents WILL PRESERVE a copy on file in their office.

$800.00 Reward!

ARREST STAGE ROBBER!

1.

On the 3d of August, 1877, the stage from Fort Ross to Russian River was stopped by one man, who took from the Express box about $300, coin, and a check for $305.52, on Grangers' Bank of San Francisco, in favor of Fisk Bros. The Mail was also robbed. On one of the Way Bills left with the box the Robber wrote as follows:—

> "I've labored long and hard for bread—
> For honor and for riches—
> But on my corns too long you've trod,
> You fine haired sons of bitches.
> BLACK BART, the P o 8.

Driver, give my respects to our friend, the other driver; but I really had a notion to hang my old disguise hat on his weather eye." (*fac simile.*)

Respectfully B - B

It is believed that he went to the Town of Guerneville about daylight next morning.

2.

About one year after above robbery, July 25th, 1878, the Stage from Quincy to Oroville was stopped by one man, and W., F. & Co's box robbed of $379, coin, one Diamond Ring, (said to be worth $200) one Silver Watch, valued at $25. The Mail was also robbed. In the box, when found next day, was the following, (*fac simile*):—

> here I lay me down to sleep
> to wait the coming morrow
> perhaps success perhaps defeat
> And everlasting sorrow
> I've labored long and hard for bread
> for honor and for riches
> But on my corns too long you've tred
> You fine haired sons of bitches
> let come what will I'll try it on
> My condition cant be worse
> And if there's money in that Box
> Tis munny in my purse
> Black Bart
> the Po8

Typical reward poster for Black Bart and the note which he passed to the driver of the Sonora-Milton stagecoach. Credit photo Wells-Fargo Bank History Room, San Francisco.

Several months later Mrs. Boles received word that he and several companions had been killed by Indians. She then joined her parents in Missouri.

However, in 1874, the errant husband was seen in San Antonio at the horse races. He apparently was well-to-do; dressed in a round Derby hat, a natty suit, and swinging a cane, he stood by the rail talking to an acquaintance to whom he vouched the information that he was going to California and set up a business for himself. He was a shy, soft-spoken individual, and unlike most of the sporting fraternity; never packed a gun or joined in their games of chance or drinking hard liquor. Boles apparently was too skittish a man to stand the rough frontier and soon departed.

In 1875 we find him a resident of San Francisco, living under the alias of Charles E. Bolton or Boulton, stock broker and wealthy mine owner, whose habit was to leave the city at intervals to inspect his various mines in upper California and Nevada.

The year of 1876 was a suspicious one for Mr. Bolton, whose "mines" were apparently paying fat dividends, but strange to say, while Mr. Boulton was absent, the Wells-Fargo Company was losing money.

The stagecoach plying between San Juan and Marysville was held up, Dec. 28, 1875, with the express box and mail bags being looted again about the middle of April. Then on June 2, 1876, came another holdup of the stagecoach near Cottonwood Peak, where the robber secured a rich haul. The stage drivers, Mike Hogan and A. C. Adams, said the robberies were committed by the same man, a lone bandit whose face was concealed by a flour sack drawn over his shoulders, and his body covered by a long gray duster, all that was visible being the man's eyes, which showed through two slits in the sack for eyeholes. The robber was very quiet and courteous, and assured the driver, Al Adams, that no harm would befall him if he obeyed instructions. Having rifled the strong box and mail bags the robber slithered in to the brush and disappeared.

No further holdups occurred for the balance of 1876, then on August 3, 1877, as the Point Arena-Duncan Mills line stage jounced along the brush-lined trail, a lone bandit leaped from the bushes, a double-barreled shotgun covered the driver, and a command of "Hands Up" caused the driver to slam on his brakes and obey. Ordering the driver to turn his back or be shot down, the bandit broke open the strong box, rifled the mail bags, and disappeared into the bushes. As soon as the coast was

clear the driver leaped onto the box, and sent his horses at break-neck speed into town, where he notified the law. The sheriff and his posse quickly reached the scene of the holdup, and began a search. On a waybill of the express company the robber had scrawled a note in these lines:

I've labored long and hard for bread,
For honor, and for riches,
But on my corns, too long you've tread,
You slick haired sons of bitches.

BLACK BART, the P.O. 8 . . .

Although the lawmen did not catch the robber, they now at least had a name, one that was to plague them for several years. The miscreant robber left plain tracks into Guerneville; there all traces were lost. The note and the name attached were all that they had uncovered. Again the mine owner Charles E. Bolton had been absent from his office, but none suspected.

On July 25, 1878, as the stage running between Quincy and Oroville was approaching the Berry Creek crossing, the lone bandit again emerged from nowhere, and covering the driver, ordered him to throw down the treasure box and mail bags. The driver obeyed and was then ordered to unhitch his horses and drive them to the back of the coach. The robber then took the cash and valuables from the stong box, slit open the mail bags and did likewise. Once again he had struck the line. Before leaving the scene he scrawled these lines:

Let come what will, I'll try it on,
My condition can't be worse,
But if there's munny in the box,
It's munny in my purse.

BLACK BART, the P.O. 8 . . .

Although the writing was plainly disguised it was likewise as plainly that of an educated man.

On July 30th the bandit again put in his appearance. It was early morning and the stage driver whistled cheerfully as he neared a turn on the trail between LaPorte and Butte. Just as the stage made the turn, the bandit halted it and driver Dan Barry found himself covered by a shotgun. Once more the stage was filched and the robber took to the woods. No trace could be found by the law when it arrived upon the scene. On October 2, 1878, a stage was stopped twelve miles from Ukiah on the Cahto-Ukiah run. Still seeking more loot, the robber struck again the following day; this time on the Cavelo-Potter-Ukiah line. The posse, which was soon after on the the trail, picked up tracks lead-

$1,000

Reward for the Apprehension of

BLACK BART, Po8

Perpetrator of the following Verses

THE COLLECTED WORKS OF

here I lay me down to Sleep
to wait the coming morrow
perhaps Success, perhaps defeat
And everlasting sorrow
I've labored long and hard for bread
for honor and for riches
But on my corns too long you've tred
You fine haired sons of Bitches
let come what will I'll try it on
My condition can't be worse
and if there's money in that Box
Tis munny in my purse

                    Black Bart
                    The Po8

This is my way to get money and bread
    When I have a chance, why should I refuse
I'll not need either when I'm dead   [it?
    And I only rob those who are able to lose it

                    Placer Democrat, Auburn, n. d.

I rob the rich to feed the poor
    Which hardly is a sin:
A widow ne'er knocked at my door
    But what I let her in.
So blame me not for what I've done
    I don't deserve your curses
And if for any cause I'm hung
    Let it be for my verses.

                    S.F. Chronicle, May 26, 1954

Here I lay, while wind and rain
    Set the trees a-sobbing,
To risk my life for a damned old stage
    That isn't worth the robbing.

Lo! here I've stood, while wind and rain
    Have set the trees a-sobbin
And risked my life for that ——— stage
    That wasn't worth the robbin'.

                    Black Bart, Po8.

Goodbye Shasta County, I will bid you adieu.
May emigrate to Hell, but I'll never come back to you.

AMBROSE BIERCE ON BLACK BART'S RELEASE FROM SAN QUENTIN

Welcome, Black Bart, as you have served your term,
    And found the joy of crime to be a fiction,
I hope you'll hold your present faith, stand firm,
    And not again be open to conviction.

Your sins, though scarlet once, are now as wool!
    You've made atonement for all past offences,
And conjugated — 'T was an awful pull, —
    The verb 'to pay' in all its moods and tenses.

You were a dreadful criminal! — By Heaven,
    I think there never was a man so sinful!
We've all a pinch or two of Satan's leaven,
    But you appeared to have an even skinful.

Earth shuddered with derision at your name;
    Rivers fled backward, gravitation scorning;
The sea and sky from thinking on your shame
    Grew lobster-red at eve and in the morning.

But still, red-handed at your horrid trade,
    You wrought, to reason deaf, and to compassion.
But now with gods and men your peace is made:
    I beg you to be good and in the fashion.

What's that? — you "ne'er again will rob a stage"?
    What! did you so? Faith, I didn't know it.
Was that what threw poor Themis in a rage?
    I thought you were convicted as a poet.

I own it was a comfort to my soul,
    And soothed it better than the deepest curses,
To think they'd got one poet in a hole,
    Where, though he wrote, he could not print his verses.

I thought that Welcker, Lyon, Brooks, and all
    The ghastly crew who always are begriming
With villain couplets every page and wall,
    Might be arrested and "run in" for rhyming.

And then Parnassus would be left to me,
    And Pegasus should bear me up it gaily,
Nor down a steep place run into the sea,
    As now he must be tempted to do daily.

So grab the lyre-strings, hearties, and begin:
    Bawl your harsh souls all out upon the gravel,
I must endure you, for you'll never sin
    By robbing coaches, until dead men travel.

                    S.F. Examiner, Jan. 29, 1888

Another reward poster for the elusive Black Bart, along with some of his terrible poetry. Credit photo Wells-Fargo Bank.

ing into Colusa, but there they lost all traces of the bold robber.

In picturing a holdup of a western stage, on one's mind runs the idea of the robber baron dashing upon the stage, his pistol or rifle covering the driver and ordering him to halt. Having completed his work, the robber then makes his escape, perhaps just ahead of a posse which follows him, sending lethal lead in his direction. Black Bart, however, was a unique operator. He never was known to ride a horse or use other means of transportation than his own two legs, and his ability to cover long distances was remarkable. He could set out at a fast walk and keep going for as much as fifty miles or more at a stretch before calling a halt.

With two holdups, one after the other, with only a day apart, the top man of the Wells-Fargo Company took charge. With a score of his operators he combined the district for several miles, and this systematic search paid off. At a remote ranch one of his men was informed that a stranger dressed in miner's garb had stopped there for food. A minute description was provided: A man of average height, lean body and wide shoulders, weight about 150 pounds, his eyes a light gray and deep set, heavy eyebrows, black hair sprinkled with gray, and a heavy mustache and imperial. The man had no visible weapons. On his shoulders he packed only a blanket roll. This description was circulated by Wells-Fargo detective J. B. Hume; then all he could do was patiently await results.

With the approach of Fall, Mr. Bolton returned to his San Francisco address and was found in his usual haunts. He was a fastidious dresser; white shirt, black tie, well pressed dark clothes, and on his head wore a little round Derby hat often called a dice box. A silk handkerchief peeked from his breast pocket, and with a walking stick he would stroll about the streets. Although living at the Webb House, Mr. Bolton took his meals at a neighborhood restaurant, which also was patronized by police officers and newspaper reporters. While partaking of his luncheon he could overhear the conversations carried on by other guests, and as Black Bart was a top subject he avidly absorbed all the latest news as to what was being done regarding the elusive bandit.

June of 1879 arrived and Charles E. Bolton, as was his custom, closed his office, and took his usual tour of inspection of his "mines." June 21st arrived with Black Bart halting stage driver Dave Quadlin on the line running between LaPorte and Oroville, securing his loot and doing his usual disappearing act. Four months later on October 25th, the Roseburg-Redding stage was held up and robbed. Two days after the bandit struck again. This time he hit the Alturas-Redding line stage and again made good his escape. Leaving the scene, this remarkable walker covered a distance of fifty miles before pausing, and having again eluded his pursurers, he reached home, and November saw him going about his usual business at his San Francisco address.

All winter he remained in town, but then with the arrival of July, 1880, he again went on his usual tour of "inspection." His first inspection was contained in the Wells-Fargo box driver M. K. McLennan carried on his stage running the Point Arena-Duncan Mills line. As the stage neared Henry Station, Black Bart, like a Jack-in-the-box, appeared upon the scene. The stage was halted as usual by a lone figure standing in the middle of the road. On the stage at this time were two residents of San Francisco, a man and his wife. This time, however, the bandit had confederates for several guns were to be seen poked through the bushes, and the tips of hats visible. Calling on his cohorts to cover him, the bandit ordered the driver to throw down the strong box and to remain quiet. He then broke open the box; slit the mail bags, and having procured the contents, he waved the stage on its journey. Black Bart did not in any manner disturb the passengers, who quietly watched his proceedings. The stage again on its way, the bandit stepped into the foliage, and removed a half dozen black painted broom handles and old hats, which had been set upon sticks, and which had served as his "confederates." Once again the baffled lawmen scoured the neighborhood, but found no trace of the robber "band."

The first day of September, 1880, Black Bart again took up his vocation. Driver Charles Cramer of the Weaverville-Redding line was held up and the stage box looted. Black Bart then headed into a ranch yard in Shasta County, and at the house secured food; then worked his way into Tehama County and disappeared. Two weeks later he had traveled north almost to the Oregon line, where he held up the Roseburg-Yreka line stage as driver Nort Eddings traveled south. Pickings must have been good for he remained in that neighborhood until January of 1881, during which time he robbed the Redding-Roseburg stage operated by Joe Mason on November 20, 1880. His hunting season then over, the man worked his way south and reached his usual haunts in San Francisco.

BLACK BART, A MAN & A LEGEND
Disguised with a flour sack over
his hard hat and armed with a
shotgun, Black Bart held-up Wells-
Fargo stages carrying gold. A the
scene of the hold-up he would
leave some verses. Trapped by a
laundry mark, Black Bart served
a short prison sentence. Upon his
release, he disappeared from
public life, and nothing further
is known of him.
The above is a photograph of
Black Bart & his signature.

Black Bart, a man and a legend disguised with a flour sack over his hard hat and armed with a shotgun, Black Bart held up Wells-Fargo stages carrying gold. At the scene of the holdup he would leave some verses. Trapped by a laundry mark, Black Bart served a short prison sentence. Upon his release he disappeared from public life. The above is a photograph of Black Bart and his signature. Credit photo Wells-Fargo Bank.

Apparently Black Bart had drawn a sizeable sum from his investment of time spent the past winter for he did not leave home until later than usual.

On August 31, 1881, he appeared back in the same area where he had spent the previous winter. He inspected his first "mine" which came traveling along the route of the Roseburg-Yreka stage line. Driver John Lulloway was stopped and ordered to rest, while the highwayman looked over his valuables. On October 8th the Yreka-Redding stage operated by Horace Williams was intercepted as it neared Bass Station on the stage line. Black Bart carried out his usual procedure; rifled the strong box and disappeared. Just three days later he struck again, holding up the Lakeview-Redding stage driven by Louis Brewster as he drove his stage up the grade of Round Mountain. The gunny-sacked head and the long gray duster were now familiar sights, and the driver discreetly did not offer any resistance. A large posse was organized but with no results, as usual. The indefatigable legs of Black Bart had been so well brought up that they couldn't bear to see him captured, and they had transported him deep into Butte County, where all trace of him vanished.

The 15th of December, 1881, witnessed the robbing of the stage plying the Downieville-Marysville route, and operated by George Sharpe. Again Black Bart disappeared, but was back on the job again December 27th, to rob the stage on the North San Juan-Smartsville line, and securing a good haul, after which he departed from Yuba County. When January of 1882 was drawing to a close Black Bart closed his nefarious crimes for the time being by robbing the Ukiah-Cloverdale line stage on January 26th. As was the case in all other robberies, driver Harry Forse could give no helpful information. A posse tracked the bandit as far as Kelseyville, and he was seen near Colusa at a later date, but escaped.

The middle of June saw Black Bart again on the job. He began his season's work by robbing the stage of Thomas B. Forse near Little lake on the 14th. His next attempt was on July 13th, when despite this unlucky date he picked upon the stage of George Helms, plying between LaPorte and Oroville. This line, having been held up on several occasions, had installed a shotgun messenger to protect the Express Company's money. When Black Bart leaped into the road he met resistance for the first time in his career. With the bandit's call to halt, the messenger went into action; George W. Hackett sending a load of buckshot winging at the highwayman. Black Bart lost all

interest in the strong box and mail, and lit a shuck as fast as his legs could carry him into the bushes. The stage was carrying a large amount of money, and the driver did not tarry in the neighborhood, but drove full speed into town, and a posse was soon after the robber. Black Bart did not make his usual speed it appears, as the posse was at one time so close to him that he took refuge in a hollow log, where he remained until the coast was clear. A Derby hat was found by the posse, in which several holes made by buckshot were discovered.

Black Bart remained quiet until the middle of September of 1882 before starting up again, then up in Shasta County he held up the stage of Horace Williams about a dozen miles from Yreka. After taking the valuables from the strong box Black Bart requested the driver to convey his respects to J. B. Hume, a special agent of the Wells-Fargo Company.

Black Bart's compliments to J. B. Hume were duly delivered, and at a later date Mr. Hume returned them to him by placing Black Bart behind prison bars.

On November 24, 1882, Black Bart struck the stage line some six miles out of Cloverdale on the Lakeport-Cloverdale line. The driver, Ed Crawford, quickly reached town and a posse took the trail, which led toward Lower Lake, where the posse sighted the bandit, but this vigorous walker was too much for the posse, and he outdistanced the men on horseback.

Black Bart opened his 1883 season by robbing the stage of driver Connibeck on the Lakeport-Cloverdale line on April 12th. He forced the driver to unhitch his horses and to drive them some distance behind the stage. Black Bart then rifled the strong box; took to the brush and again made good his escape.

June found him in Amador County, where, on the 23rd, he held up the stage of Clint Radcliffe on the Jackson-Lone City line. His haul packed in his duster, he went his merry way, and from a distance watched the disgruntled lawmen chase themselves around the scene of the holdup; then head back to town. Bart seemed to be anxious to get in his winter supply of gold for on November 3, 1883, he was prepared for the stage from Sonora, Calaveras County, as it topped a grade in the trail, or perhaps he was cognizant that it carried a good amount of dinero. At any rate, as the stage approached a huge boulder, Black Bart suddenly appeared and ordered the driver to halt, then unhitch his animals and place them some distance back of the stalled stage. The strong box

Stagecoach arriving, Mother Lode, painting by Louis Macouillard. Credit photo Wells-Fargo Bank History Room, San Francisco.

Beneath the driver's seat of the Wells-Fargo Stage rode the treasure box, containing placer washings, gold dust, and quartz ore. Countless millions in raw gold and bullion were carried all over the West on Wells-Fargo stages. Credit photo Wells-Fargo Bank History Room, San Francisco.

was on the ground, Black Bart proceeded to break the lock with an axe, and a smile crossed his face as he lifted $5,000 from the box, and was about to make his departure when a bullet sped past his head. Without a moment's hesitation, the little highwayman took to his heels, his booty under his arm. With his departure a youth of around sixteen years of age approached the driver. He was a boy living in the neighborhood, who with his .22 calibre rifle, had been out hunting, and seeing the masked man and the unhitched teams, had surmised the reason and come to the driver's aid.

Meanwhile, Black Bart cached his ill gotten gains in a hollow stump and made tracks out of the district. In his rush to get away he left his Derby hat and his linen handkerchief, which had become caught on a twig. These small and insignificant pieces of wearing apparel were to prove his downfall. Driver McConnell hitched up his horses, then burned the breeze for Copperopolis and gave the news.

Within a short time of Black Bart's departure the posse under Sheriff Ben Thorne of Calaveras County appeared upon the scene, and the Derby hat and the handkerchief were discovered. Also near the spot where the robber had stood when fired upon was found a pair of field glasses. Detective John N. Thacker of the Wells-Fargo Company, also was in the posse, and when he examined the handkerchief he knew that here was the most valuable clue picked up so far. On the piece of linen was a laundry mark "FXO-7." The evidence was then placed in the hands of Special Agent J. B. Hume of the Wells-Fargo Company, the same man to whom Black Bart had conveyed his greetings via a stage driver, and who also had been working on the case for several years. Detective Hume then called in his assistants, Harry N. Morse and John N. Thacker, for a consultation.

"There seems little chance of this laundry mark being used by any small town laundry men, so we'll concentrate upon San Francisco first," remarked the chief.

Each operator on Hume's staff was assigned a certain district, with instructions to canvass every place where washing was done, private or large laundries, and slowly but surely the detectives covered their assignments, all anxious to see the robber run to earth. By this time Black Bart had rewards out for his capture, amounting to $18,000. Detective Morse had about run out of places, his men had visited almost a hundred laundries without results, when Morse reached a tobacco shop run by T. C. Ware on Bush Street, who also acted as agent for a laundry concern. When shown the laundry mark, he had no difficulty in tracing it to a customer named Charles E. Bolton.

"Sure I know Mr. Bolton; he is a mining man, owns mines in Nevada and California, and goes there every summer to inspect his property," vouched the storekeeper.

The men were still in conversation when Mr. Ware suddenly looked out the window and exclaimed, "There he is now."

Charles E. Bolton was just passing the store on his way to the Webb House located at 73 Second Street. Mr. Ware called Bolton into the store, and introduced the two men.

"Mr. Ware tells me you are a mining man, Mr. Bolton, and an expert on ore. I have a number of specimens in my office, and would appreciate it if you could accompany me there and examine them for me."

Mr. Bolton and the detective then headed downtown together. Down Bush Street to Montgomery, thence via California Street, they reached 320 Sansome Street, where they entered and proceeded into an office ... the office of Special Agent J. B. Hume, Black Bart's nemesis. Bolton then realized that he had stepped into a trap, but he lost none of his nerve. Detective Hume wasted no time in preliminaries, and stepping to a hat rack proceeded to take from it a small Derby hat, which he extended toward Mr. Bolton, with a request that he try it on.

Charles E. Bolton, nonchalantly complied and then remarked, "It fits me, sir, do you wish to sell it?"

"I would hardly feel justified in trying to sell you a hat which already belongs to you, sir," replied Hume.

In the meanwhile a detective with a search warrant had ransacked Bolton's room, and soon appeared in the office, and delivered a bundle which contained a double-barrel shotgun, unbreeched, a gray linen duster, and an old Bible, in which appeared the name of Charles E. Boles, and which was the man's real name, the Bible had been given to him by his wife while he was in the army. With such indisputable evidence placed before him, the man at last gave in and admitted that he was the culprit, Black Bart.

"We have your shotgun, Mr. Bolton; where do you keep your ammunition?" asked Hume.

A smile flitted across Bolton's face as he replied, "Gentlemen, I never owned any. In all my holdups my gun was always empty. After serving in the army, and seeing what a lot of misery a gun could bring to humanity I swore never again to fire a gun as long as I lived, and I have kept that vow!"

Black Bart having confessed his robberies, then agreed to take the officers back to the scene of the last holdup, and did so, and in the hollow stump they found the haul of $5,000 which he had taken. During the period of over seven years that Black Bart had operated it is claimed that he got away with the total sum of $50,000, but all that the company ever did recover was this sum of $5,000. He also admitted that when he had first gone to California, he had worked in the mines at Butte, El Dorado, Shasta, and in Trinity Counties, and thus being well acquainted with that district had chosen it for his field of operations.

Taken to Mohelumne Hill, where he had robbed a stage, Black Bart was arraigned in the Superior Court, and on his plea of guilty as charged, was sentenced to serve six years in the San Quentin Prison. He was received at the California State Prison from Calaveras County on November 21, 1883, for the offense of robbery. When he was admitted to the prison as convict No. 11046 Black Bart was 48 years old, 5 feet 7 inches tall, with blue eyes and grey hair. He was released from custody on January 21, 1888.

Black Bart had proved a model prisoner, and when released from prison he returned to San Francisco, where he called upon Captain John Thacker, chief of the Wells-Fargo detective force.

"What are your future plans, Mr. Bolton?" asked Thacker.

"I'm going straight. I found out that crime does not pay," replied Bart.

"Are you going to write more poetry?"

"Hell no!" emphatically replied Black Bart. "I swore I wouldn't commit any more crimes, didn't I?"

Many reports were circulated that Black Bart was paid a monthly pension by the Wells-Fargo people on his promise not to rob any more of their stages.

There are some researchers who claim that Boles was not Black Bart's real name, although that name was on the fly-leaf of the Bible found in his room. He had been known as Barlow, Spaulding, Bolton or Boulton, and the mystery of his parentage has never been satisfactorily solved.

Black Bart left behind for posterity a romantic interest, one which keeps alive even after a lapse of nearly a hundred years. Leaving San Francisco, he traveled to Japan, Alaska, and Mexico, and finally returned to his birthplace in New York, where he died in 1917.

Although Black Bart had secured thousands of dollars during his career of crime, he did not have a penny left when his prison term ended. He was a sucker for scheming stock manipulators, where most of his money went. It was also reliably testified that much of it went to the poor, who lived in the districts where he worked as a robber, and that in return these people sheltered and fed him between holdups, and gave misleading information as to the direction he had taken. In this manner Black Bart was able to evade the law for many years before his apprehension.

There has been no parallel in the history of crime which can compare with that of the career of Charles E. Boles. Robbing numerous stage-coaches with an unloaded gun, and escaping each time without the aid of a horse, using only his two feet to cover great distances in a short time. Seven years a holdup artist without firing one shot; then being run to earth by means of a handkerchief. He had a deathly fear of horses!

There was a little man, who owned a little gun,
He had no lead to load it, just carried it for fun,
He'd use it to stop a stage, and drivers acted smart,
And when his gun; he displayed, they always minded Bart.

THE END

Wells-Fargo Stage Traveling over one of the treacherous roads while making their daily runs. Credit photo Worden Collection, Wells-Fargo Bank History Room.

Riding shotgun on a U. S. Mail stage. The shotgun messenger was armed with a double-barrel shotgun and often carried a Wells-Fargo Colt, a pocket pistol designed 1849 for use by express guards and police. Credit photo Wells-Fargo Bank History Room, San Francisco.

One of the many stages that plied the wilderness trails in Placer County, Calif., and the type that Black Bart held up. Credit photo Wells-Fargo Bank History Room, San Francisco.

(Above) Departure from Cheyenne, Wyoming T., of the last coach of the Black Hills Stage Line. Railroad vs. Stagecoach. The New Epoch in the History of the Northwest, from photos by C. D. Kirkland, Cheyenne, Wyo. T. Credit photo Wells-Fargo Bank. (Below) The vehicle which was to play such a vital part in the history of Wells-Fargo, and of the West, was a product of Yankee ingenuity build by Abbott-Downing Co. of Concord, New Hampshire. Most of Wells-Fargo's coaches were ordered from this firm. The Concord Coach weighed 2500 pounds and cost $1250.00. Credit photo Wells-Fargo Bank.

Panoramic view of San Francisco. Credit photo California State Library, San Francisco.

Detective James B. Hume, Chief of Detectives for Wells-Fargo Company, and the man who finally captured Black Bart through a laundry mark on his handkerchief left at the scene of one of his daring robberies. Credit photo Wells-Fargo Bank History Room, San Francisco.

Shotgun used by Black Bart — was never loaded.

THE AUTHORS

Carl W. Breihan is a former St. Louis County Police Commissioner. He lives with his wife Ethel and daughter Janis Sue in Mattese, Mo., a suburban area of St. Louis. He also has a son Carl, Jr. and a married daughter Carol Ann.

The author is historian and consultant for the Jesse James Territory tourist attraction at Sullivan, Missouri, an hour's drive from St. Louis on Hwy. 66. It is a reproduction of an 1880 Missouri town, complete with steam train, simulated shootouts and hangings.

Colonel Breihan is employed by the George Miller Chevrolet Company and spends a great deal of time in his writings, as well as being a member of the St. Louis County Council. He is now working on a biography of Quantrill.

Charles Rosamond writes that he has had a life long urge to find the goodness in man. Perhaps he prefers a quest with a real challenge. Whatever prompted the urge it is the editor's thought that he has searched in strange places; Henry Starr, Jesse James, the Youngers, Wild Bill Hickock and others.

Be that as it may he has undoubtably had much pleasure over a period of 26 years, travelling old trails, researching interesting fact and legend about the bad men of the old West.

BIBLIOGRAPHY

Hell on the Border, S. W. Harman, Phoenix Publishing Co., 1898, Fort Smith, Arkansas.

Calamity Jane and Other Lady Wildcats, Duncan Aikman, Henry Holt & Co., New York, 1927.

Tulsa, A Guide to the Oil Capital, Federal Writers' Project, Midwest Printing Company, Tulsa, Oklahoma, 1938.

Muskogee & Northeastern Oklahoma, John D. Benedict, S. J. Clarke Publishing Co., Chicago, Illinois, Vol. 1, 1922.

Belle Starr, the Bandit Queen, William Yancey Shackelford, Haldemann-Julius Publishing Co., Girard, Kansas, 1943.

Belle Starr, the Bandit Queen, Burton Rascoe, Random House, New York, 1941.

The Story of Cole Younger, Cole Younger, Henneberry Co., Chicago, Illinois, 1903.

True Facts of the Lives of America's Most Notorious Outlaws, Scout Younger Pamphlet.

The Story of Oklahoma, Muriel H. Wright, Webb Publishing Co., Oklahoma City, Oklahoma, 1930; Assisted editorially by Jos. B. Thoburn.

The Red River Valley, Then and Now, A. W. Neville, Carl Hertzog, Paris, Texas, 1948.

Oklahombres, Everitt Dumas Nix, Eden Publishing House, St. Louis, Missouri, 1929.

A Treasury of Western Folklore, B. A. Botkin, Crown Publishing Co., New York, 1951.

The Founding of Stillwater, Berlin Basil Chapman, Times Journal Publishing Co., Oklahoma City, Oklahoma, 1948.

California, A Guide to the Golden State, Federal Writers' Project, Hastings House, New York.

U. S. West, the Saga of Wells Fargo, Lucius Beebe & Charles Clegg, E. P. Dutton Publishing Co., New York, 1949.

My Playhouse was a Concord Coach, Mae Bacon Boggs, Howell-North Press, Oakland, California, 1942.

Pioneer Days of Angel's Camp, Edna B. Buckbee, Calaveras Californian, 1932.

Catalogue of Wells Fargo Company, H. S. Crocker Co., 1893.

Wells Fargo Bank History Room, San Francisco, California

Oklahoma State Historical Society

California State Historical Society

Personal papers and album of the Shirley family, Chas. Rosamond.

The Arkansas, Clyde Brion Davis, Farrar & Rinehart, New York, 1940.

Hanging Judge, Fred Harvey Harrington, Caxton Printers, Ltd., Caldwell, Idaho, 1951.

INDEX